ROMAN COOKERY's 360 easy-to-follow recipes
show how to prepare delectable, poetic dishes from classical
Rome, from simple snacks to complete dinners. As one reviewer
said: "Makes Roman cooking completely accessible to us in our day,
with proportions of foods and seasonings which are pleasing to
the contemporary palate. Only the great gods know what proportions
pleased the Romans, but Edwards has wisely decided to please us."
These recipes, using natural ingredients available to anyone,
astonish us with their refreshing combinations, and provide
a delicious variety of flavors without once
resorting to the use of salt.

### FRONT COVER DISHES (Clockwise)

*Celery Seed Sauce for Prawns,* page 208
*Broccoli in Coriander Wine Sauce,* page 26
*Spiced Pork Hors D'oeuvres Apicius,* page 102
*Hot Salmon Fish-Pickle,* page 2
*Spiced Wine Apicius,* page 4
*Potted Salad Apicius,* page 40
*Mussels in Savory Wine,* page 175
*Pears Cooked with Cinnamon Wine Cream,* page 55
*"Peppered" Sweet Cakes,* page 117

Part of a highly desirable new trend to make classic cookbooks available to the general public. —*Vogue*

The sort of dishes that wouldn't be out of place in *The Joy of Cooking*. No average cookbook—quite simply, delicious. —*Edmonton Journal*

I like it very much, have used many of the recipes, and I think the present treatment is an excellent one in every way. —*M. F. K. Fisher*

Makes Roman cooking completely accessible to us in our day, [with] proportions of foods and seasonings which are pleasing to the contemporary palate. Only the great gods know what proportions pleased the Romans, but Edwards has wisely decided to please us. . . . An intriguing blend of the ancient and the 80's. —*Classical Views*

Imaginative, daring, lively, and literary, a first-class cookbook. —*Booksellers Choice* prize-winner (Canada).

The best of Italian kitchens, even when not in Rome. —*Homemakers Magazine*

Early Roman recipes updated in compelling style. One of the most interesting cookbooks to be published in recent memory. —*Columbus Dispatch*

A treasure. —*Vancouver Courier*

A perfect gift. —*Seattle-Post-Intelligence*

A roaring success. —*Books in Canada*

Edwards' adaptations rein in the Roman excesses, and fare far better in our kitchens than the originals. Many, such as his delicious nut sauce for duck, show what a little restrained spicing can do. —*Toronto Globe & Mail*

A fascinating glimpse into the foodstyle of ancient Rome. —*Attenzione*

# Roman Cookery

## Elegant & Easy Recipes from History's First Gourmet

*Revised Edition*

*by JOHN EDWARDS*

Hartley & Marks, Publishers

*Produced by*
*Hartley and Marks, Ltd.*

*Published in the U.S.A. by*
*Hartley & Marks, Inc.,*
*P.O. Box 147, Point Roberts*
*Washington*
*98281*

*Published in Canada by*
*Hartley & Marks, Ltd.,*
*3663 West Broadway*
*Vancouver, B.C.*
*V6R 2B8*

*Printed in the U.S.A.*

ISBN 0-88179-011-7

*Typeset by The Typeworks*
*Cover photographs by Sue Tauber*

Library of Congress Cataloging-in-Publication Data

*Apicius.*
*Roman cookery.*

*Translation of: De re coquinaria.*
*Includes index.*
1. Cookery, Roman—Early works to 1800.
I. Edwards, John, 1946–  .  II. Title.
TX713.A6413 1986    641.5937    86–25609
ISBN 0-88179-011-7 *(pbk.)*

# ACKNOWLEDGEMENTS

Of the various existing texts, I wish to express my admiration for the one edited by Mary Ella Milham, published in the Teubner collection, Leipzig, 1969. Her *De Re Coquinaria*, together with the alternate readings she supplies, have been enormously valuable to me as the foundation and touchstone upon which I built a practical translation and commentary for use in the modern kitchen.

André's Latin-French dual text, *L'Art Culinaire* (1965) supplies a clear French translation of Apicius and Vinidarius, and has been helpful to me as an example of comparative translation. Many of André's Latin readings were later confirmed by Milham. In some instances I chose André's reading over Milham's.

The Latin-English text, *The Roman Cookery Book* (1958), by Flower and Rosenbaum, uses the Giarratano-Vollmer text and contains a number of interesting speculations upon the nature of classical Roman cookery.

Vehling's *Cookery and Dining in Imperial Rome* (republished in 1977) is a fascinating and personal treatment of the *De Re Coquinaria*. Vehling refers frequently and in lively language to earlier students of Apicius. His translation is based upon texts by Torinus, Humelbergius, Lister, and Giarratano-Vollmer. Unfortunately, numerous interpolations and bracketed words make his text very difficult to read. However, his commentary contains valuable insights for the practical use of the *De Re Coquinaria*.

I also wish to acknowledge the encouragement of my mother, Betty Edwards, and the enormous support of my wife, Gillian, both in the kitchen and out of it, and the late Professor Edith Wightman, in whose house I first tasted an Apician meal. Lastly, I am very grateful to my editor, Sue Tauber, for her faith in the book, and for her painstaking and tasteful editorial skills.

*I dedicate this book
to the memory of my father and mentor,
Newton Edwards.*

# CONTENTS

# Contents

# IT'S EASY TO BE A ROMAN CHEF

This book is nothing less than the adapted recipes of the famous gourmet Apicius, using the secrets of ancient Roman and classical Greek cuisine to enliven our modern tables. Roman cookery is delicious and not difficult. We today eat the same green vegetables, meats, poultry, and, with one or two exceptions due to over-fishing, the same seafood as the classical Europeans. Though they cooked in metal and clay on charcoal and wood stoves, and we use electricity or gas, the difference is only one of convenience. Most of the spices we enjoy are identical to theirs—not surprisingly—since the Greeks and Romans popularized them in the first place. They introduced the West to pepper, cinnamon, nutmeg, and cloves through the expansion of their sea trade routes into Asia. As for the herbs beloved by Apicius and the Mediterranean schools of classical cookery, they are growing right now in my garden. There are mints, celery seed, savory, rosemary, rue, lovage, thyme, oregano, sage, and parsley. I can buy coriander, cumin, aniseed, and juniper in the local supermarket, and nearly any other Roman seasoning, with the single exception of lovage. This leafy herb's flavor can be imitated by celery seed or celery leaves. Lovage thrives in our cool, rainy, coastal climate, and once a few seeds are thrown into the soil it is difficult *not* to grow it.

In fact, where good cooking is concerned, language is the only obvious difference between us and the Romans of two thousand years ago. There is, though, a difference of style. Apicius based his famous sauces on the balance between crushed green herbs and ground spices. Lovage (or celery leaves), oregano, and thyme, for example, are matched by pepper, cumin, and coriander. To these seasonings he added a second level of flavors, the sweetness of a little honey and the sourness of a spoonful of vinegar. There are numerous quickly made sauces and broths using a variety of such ingredients which entirely transform simply prepared meats or seafoods. In slightly more elaborate recipes he used a third element: raisins, dates, or plums appear beside almonds, walnuts, or chestnuts. Then everything is cooked in the wine and stock appropriate for the particular meat, seafood, or vegetable. Today we can dress up many ordinary meats or seafoods just by using these sauces. Nothing could be easier than drenching some precooked chicken meats or shrimps after a long day at work, and dining in delicious Roman splendor.

Of course, there are also very festive dishes, in some cases with rich stuffings, which echo the composition of the sauces. Herbs, spices, fruits, and nuts season ground meats and bread crumbs, and all are bound with egg, and cooked inside poultry, suckling lamb, or kid. These have their place today when we entertain or want to indulge ourselves a little.

Variations and substitutions on this theme of balance and harmony are found everywhere in these recipes, yet the basic methods are quite familiar to us. The delectable results remind me of Sappho's and Horace's lyric poems: balanced, full of subtle repetitions, and pleasant surprises. They allow us all to become poets of the kitchen.

A few words about Apicius, first century author of *De Re Coquinaria (On Cookery)* from whom all these recipes come. There is much confusion about the identity of Apicius. Three gastrophiles bore this name in Imperial Rome. The first lived during the meteoric rise of Julius Caesar (d. 44 B.C.). The second taught *haute cuisine* under Augustus and Tiberius (27 B.C.– 37 A.D.), and enjoyed the reputation of a wealthy and decadent gourmet. The third Apicius lived during the reign of Trajan (98– 117 A.D.).

> *When the Emperor Trajan was in Parthia, a journey of many days from the sea, Apicius arranged to have fresh oysters sent to him, preserved by his own skill.*
>
> Athenaeus.

It is recorded that so great was Apicius' love of food that he poisoned himself for fear of dying of hunger.

*After you'd spent 60 million on your stomach, Apicius,*
  *10 million still remained,*
*An embarrassment, you said, fit only to satisfy*
  *Mere hunger and thirst:*
*So your last and most expensive meal was poison. . . .*
  *Apicius, you never were more a glutton than at the end.*

Martial.

In fact, by the end of the first century A.D., the name "Apicius" had already become a cliché for wealth. We may amuse ourselves with the image of a man with this name delighting in his role as the arbiter of cuisine in the villas and palaces of Rome at the zenith of her wealth and power.

*The great Apicius was pleased to go out to dine:*
  *Even gourmets grow depressed at home.*

Martial.

And perhaps this was so; but no individual personality emerges from the pages of Apicius' *Cookery*. Only twice does the impersonal mask momentarily slip. On one occasion he concludes a recipe by saying enthusiastically, "You'll be amazed." On the other he ironically comments on a recipe for anchovy stew made without anchovies. *Ad mensam nemo agnoscet quid manducet.* (At the table nobody will know what he's eating.) In short, "Apicius" is best regarded as a proverbial name for the greatest and most notorious of the Roman writers on cookery. Stories of his legendary wealth and excesses abounded and he passed into history as a kind of Croesus of the kitchen.

*There lived in the reign of Tiberius a man named Apicius, a*
*voluptuary of extraordinary wealth, who gave his name to many*
*kinds of cakes. Apicius lavished countless sums of money on his stomach*
*in Minturnae, a city in Campania. There he passed his time for the*
*most part eating the very costly prawns of the region, which grow*
*larger than the biggest prawns of Smyrna or the lobsters of*
*Alexandria. He happened to hear that prawns also grew to an*
*enormous size off the coasts of Libya and accordingly set sail from Italy*

*without the delay of even a single day. After suffering from storms during the voyage across the open sea he drew near land. The Libyan fishermen sailed towards him before he had set out from his ship, for the report of his arrival had already spread, and they brought him their best prawns. Seeing these he inquired as to whether they had any that were larger. But when they replied that none grew larger than those they had offered him, Apicius suddenly remembered the prawns of his own Minturnae and commanded his helmsman to sail back to Italy by the same route they had taken to Libya, without making any further approach to land.*

Athenaeus.

In spite of Apicius' deficiencies his name gave legitimacy to successful and admired recipes, whether or not he had originally created them. His book captured for all time the essence of what was best in the art of Roman cooking, and makes an exciting discovery for food lovers today.

## ABOUT THE RECIPES

The Romans of the first century A.D. enjoyed foods which were very sweet and highly spiced. I have been moderate in my use of the herbs and spices, but Apicius' recipes easily lend themselves to experimentation, and no one version of each recipe can do justice to the wonderful combination of flavors. So do not be afraid to experiment with the herbs and spices, or by using the sauces to accompany different foods.

Apicius' recipes were not arranged in the groupings usually found in modern cookbooks. For example, you may find recipes for the same meat or fish in two or three different parts of the book instead of all in one place, as might be expected. For this reason, the index provides the best way to find a dish. Of course, simply browsing through the book is another, very pleasant way to discover the recipes.

For the curious, sample pages showing ancient recipes are scattered throughout the book.

On page 215 I have recorded the substitutes for the hard to find ingredients I have used.

The recipes for fish-pickle, which is delicious served as a spread, and also appears as an ingredient in some recipes, are found on page 2.

Page 3 contains directions for making the boiled wine, and the wine sauce, which are used as ingredients in various recipes.

Pre-packaged, commercially ground spices work perfectly well in these recipes, but if you take only two or three extra minutes to grind the needed spices with a simple mortar and pestle, you will never regret it. The resulting aromas and flavors will be much livelier and fuller than those of the bottled spices. (A small porcelain mortar and pestle cost about three dollars and can be found in most kitchenware stores, and in many shops in Chinese neighborhoods.)

The recipes, with a few obvious exceptions, are intended to provide from four to five servings.

Enjoy these meals! *Cenabis bene*—You'll dine well.

## SOME FAVORITE MODERN ROMAN MEALS

### *Luncheons or Light Dinners*

#### I

Hors d'oeuvres: Fish-pickle Cheese Hors d'oeuvres (page 119)
Main dish: Nut Omelette (page 41)
(Served with a Spinach Salad and a glass of Beer.)
*Excellent in midsummer after a morning's work in the garden. You can wake up the salad by combining finely chopped rosemary (or rue), celery leaves (or lovage), oregano, and pepper, with an oil and vinegar dressing.*

#### II

Hors d'oeuvres: Stuffed Sardines (page 175)
Main dish: Spinach (or Nettle) Quiche (page 56)
Vegetable: Chilled Peas Vinaigrette (page 71)
(For dessert, Sliced Apples, Plums, Pears, Cherries, and Strawberries with Vanilla Ice Cream.)
*A healthful yet satisfying meal. If nettles are used, they are best in the spring, before the hot sun has coarsened them. With a bottle of chilled white wine this makes a lovely intimate lunch.*

### III

Hors d'oeuvres: Lobster or Crabmeat in Cumin Sauce for
All Kinds of Shellfish (page 174)
Cold Roast Duck with Cold Sauce Apicius (page 90)
Beans Vitellian with Leeks and Fennel (page 74)
(Served with Small Buttered New Potatoes.)
Dessert: Pears (Served with Nuts) Cooked with
Cinnamon & Wine (page 55)

*An elegant meal with gentle sauces. Cinnamon is used in the dessert and
more subtly in the sauce for lobster at the beginning.*

### IV

Main dish: Lamb Chops in a Simple Sauce (page 212)
Vegetable: Squash in Oregano Wine Sauce (page 22)
(Served with a simple Salad.)
Dessert: Roman Custard (page 118)

*The coriander wine sauce in which the lamb chops are finished is
complemented by the celery seed sauce which seasons the squash. A very
simple, but very good meal.*

### *Dinners*

### I

Aperitif: Spiced Wine Apicius (page 4)
Hors d'oeuvres: Dates Alexandrine (page 117)
Main dish: Baked Salmon (or Cod) in Caraway Date Sauce (page 197)
(Served with Broccoli in a standard Cheese and Parsley Sauce.)
(For dessert, Chilled Blackberries in Wine.)

*The caraway date sauce is wonderful with salmon, and the sweetness of
the aperitif and hors d'oeuvres is echoed in the dessert by using a sweet red
wine with the blackberries.*

## II

Hors d'oeuvres: Mussel Forcemeat Sausage Canapés (page 8)
Main dish: Frontinian Pork with Anise and Chives (page 149)
(Served with Baked Potatoes and Sour Cream, and
Steamed Carrot Strips Spiced with Cumin.)
Dessert: Pears Cooked with Cinnamon and Wine (page 55)

*This dinner is among the most outstanding of Roman meals. Apicius used
cumin so skilfully that it can appear, with delicious results, in desserts
and with seafoods, as well as in main dishes.*

## III

Soup: Vegetable and Lentil Soup (page 62)
Main dish: Stuffed Roast Suckling Kid with Wine Sauce (page 145)
(Served with Boiled Small New Potatoes.)
Vegetable: Green Beans in Coriander Sauce (page 77)
(For dessert, Cheese and Assorted Nuts.)

*This is a classical feast which I make on special days, like the last day of
school. The cost and complexity of the suckling kid recipe will be repaid at
the table, where it generously serves 12 people.*

## IV

Aperitif: Cold Spiced Wine Apicius (page 4)
Hors d'oeuvres: Fish-pickle Cheese Hors d'oeuvres (page 119)
Main dish: Rabbit Stuffed with Liver and Sausage (page 156)
(Served with Steamed Squash, Boiled Small New Potatoes,
and a Spinach Salad.)
(For dessert, Trifle or Berries with Whipped Cream.)

*These dishes are perfect for a dinner party. The rabbit's stuffing is
very rich, so that the vegetables and salad are best kept simple, to set
off the main dish.*

## V

First course: Fish Stewed in Seasoned Wine (page 206)
Main dish: Chicken Vardanus with Chives and Hazelnuts (page 94)
Vegetable: Alexandrine Squash (page 21)
(Served with Mushrooms Sautéed in Butter, and Hot Rolls.)
Dessert: Chilled, Herbed Peaches with Cumin (page 54)

*Fresh, green chives and the squash make this dinner colorful as well as
delicious. A touch of cumin is the secret ingredient in the herbed peaches.*

## VI

Salad: Watercress Salad (page 32)
Main dish: Roast Duck in a Blanket of Turnips (page 81)
Vegetable: Mushrooms with Coriander (page 120)
(Served with Steamed Beans in the Pod, and Roast Potatoes.)
Dessert: Sweet Apricot Hors d'oeuvres (page 64)

*It's fun to prepare roast duck in this way, and its striking appearance
will draw applause when it is served. A fine dinner for friends who enjoy
an aesthetic adventure.*

## VII

Aperitif: Spiced Wine Apicius (page 4)
Hors d'oeuvres: Broiled Pork Liver with Bacon Slices (page 100)
Main dish: Roast Lamb in Ginger Sauce (page 143)
(Served with Steamed Brussel Sprouts and Roast Potatoes.)
(For dessert: Apples and Cheeses.)

*The spiced wine is excellent served with the hors d'oeuvres. The lamb's
ginger sauce has an Asian flavor, and recalls Rome's spice trade with the
Orient in the first century—history you can eat!*

# Roman Cookery

# The Careful Cook

## SPECIAL INGREDIENTS

### *Mild Fish-pickle*

*Delicious both as a seasoning, a relish, and used like a paté.*

*3 ounces, drained and washed, canned tuna or salmon, or* unsalted *sardines or* unsalted *anchovies*
*2 t. white wine*
*1 T. vinegar*
*½ t. mustard seed*
*½ t. oregano*
*½ t. celery seed (or lovage)*
*1 T. olive oil*
*½ t. honey*
*pinch of basil*
*¼ t. thyme*
*1 mint leaf, finely chopped*

In a mixing bowl, thoroughly combine all ingredients. This fish-pickle may be stored in the refrigerator in a glass jar for up to 2 weeks, and should then be replaced.

### *Hot Fish-pickle*

*Delicious both as a seasoning, a relish, and used like a paté.*

*3 ounces, drained and washed, canned tuna or salmon, or* unsalted *sardines or* unsalted *anchovies*
*1 T. white wine*
*1 T. vinegar*
*1 T. olive oil*
*1 small clove of garlic, crushed*
*¼ t. pepper*
*2 t. parsley*
*¼ t. rosemary, ground*
*¼ t. sage*
*1 mint leaf, finely chopped*
*pinch of basil*

In a mixing bowl, thoroughly combine all ingredients. This fish-pickle may be stored in the refrigerator in a glass jar for up to 2 weeks, and should then be replaced.

## Special Ingredients—*continued*

### *Boiled Wine*

Whenever boiled wine is indicated as an ingredient, the required quantity is obtained by bringing double the amount to a boil and simmering it till it is reduced to ½ its volume.

*Example:* To obtain ½ cup of boiled wine, boil 1 cup till it is reduced by half.

### *Wine Sauce*

Combine equal parts of wine and an appropriate stock, with olive oil or butter added, to taste.

*My cook wants a mountain of peppercorns*
*And then he'll waste my best Falernian wine*
*To make his precious fish-pickle recipe*
*And now that enormous boar he's bought*
*Won't even fit the stove: by the father of the gods*
*I swear he's trying to bankrupt me.*

Martial.

## Spiced Wine Apicius

*1 c. white wine*
*1 lb. honey*
*1 t. ground pepper*
*pinch of saffron*
*1 crushed bay leaf*
*(or spikenard)*
*1 t. cinnamon*
*(or mastic)*
*2 dates*
*3½ quarts white wine*

Served hot, this spiced wine is an excellent drink for a winter's evening. As a dinner wine, Apicius' Conditum Paradoxum should be served at room temperature with the hors d'oeuvres or at the "gustatio" (light first course of the Roman meal).

For a party of ten, use the following adapted recipe, which reduces approximately by half in cooking.

In a saucepan, combine one cup of white wine and a pound of honey. Heat and dissolve, stirring continuously. Then pour the honeyed wine into a deep pot. Add the pepper, saffron, bay leaf (or spikenard), and cinnamon (or mastic). Steep two dates in white wine, then chop them finely, and add them to the pot. Now pour the 3½ quarts of white wine into the honey and spice mixture. Simmer for one hour over low heat, stirring from time to time with a wooden spoon or spatula.

*To complement an evening of pleasant conversation, strain and serve the mulled spiced wine hot. Allow the wine to cool if it is to begin a dinner in the Roman style.*

*Prepared in this way, the spiced wine will have a subtle taste that hints of lemon.*

## Fennel Sauce for Meats

*¼ t. pepper*
*1 pinch of caraway*
*pinch of aniseed*
*2 t. parsley*
*½ t. mint*
*⅛ t. fennel*
*pinch of cinnamon*
*pinch of costmary (or mint)*
*1 bay leaf, whole*
*1 t. honey*
*1 t. white wine vinegar or*
*cider vinegar*
*1 c. beef or chicken stock*

In a mortar, grind pepper. Add to caraway, aniseed, parsley, mint, fennel, cinnamon, costmary (or mint), and bay leaf. Combine with honey, vinegar, and stock. Bring to a boil, then simmer to reduce for 25 minutes.

*A great variety of simply prepared meats can be enlivened with this sauce.*

## Truffles or Mushrooms in Coriander Wine Sauce

*peeled truffles (or mushrooms)*
*¼ t. ground pepper*
*1 t. celery seed (or lovage)*
*½ t. coriander*
*pinch of rosemary (or rue)*
*½ c. beef stock*
*½ c. red wine*
*2 t. olive oil or butter*

In a mortar, grind together pepper, celery seed (or lovage), coriander, and rosemary (or rue). Blend with stock, wine, and olive oil or butter. Bring to a boil, then simmer over low heat.

*This pungent sauce, like the one that follows, is equally good with mushrooms or truffles. Lightly cook them whole in the sauce, and serve together.*

## Truffles or Mushrooms in Savory-Thyme Sauce

*peeled truffles (or mushrooms)*
*¼ t. thyme*
*¼ t. savory*
*¼ t. ground pepper*
*¼ t. celery seed (or lovage)*
*1 t. honey*
*½ c. beef stock*
*½ c. red wine*
*2 t. olive oil or butter*

In a mortar, grind together thyme, savory, pepper, and celery seed (or lovage). Combine with honey, stock, and olive oil or butter. Mix with wine, and simmer to reduce for 25 minutes.

## Condiment Sauce with Grated Cheese

*¼ t. pepper*
*1 t. celery seed (or lovage)*
*½ t. mint*
*¼ c. pine nuts or finely chopped almonds*
*2 T. raisins*
*2 T. dates, finely chopped*
*1 t. honey*
*1 t. wine vinegar*
*1 c. beef or chicken stock*
*¼ c. white wine*
*2 T. butter*
*flour*
*½ c. mild white cheese, grated*

In a mortar, grind pepper, and celery seed (or lovage). Add to mint, nuts, raisins, and dates. Mix with honey, vinegar, stock, wine, and butter. Bring to a boil, then simmer for 20 minutes and thicken with flour.

*Sprinkle grated cheese into the sauce and serve. It is excellent with roast chicken, or game birds.*

## Country Mint Sauce

*1 T. chopped fresh mint*
*½ t. coriander*
*pinch of fennel*
*1 t. celery seed (or lovage)*
*⅛ t. ground pepper*
*2 T. honey*
*1 c. beef or chicken stock*
*1 t. wine vinegar*

Mix fresh mint with coriander, fennel, celery seed (or lovage), and pepper. Blend with honey and stock. Add vinegar to taste. Bring to a boil, then simmer gently to reduce for 25 minutes.

*This sauce is a fine complement to the flavors of roast lamb, or suckling kid, and makes even simple lamb chops into a festive dish.*

# Chopped Meats

*Forcemeats are finely chopped or ground shellfish, or meats, with the addition of spices and seasonings. They may be stuffed into sausage casings, rolled for meatballs, or used to stuff fowls or other animals. All are equally good when served as unstuffed meats.*

### Mussel Forcemeat Sausage for Two

¼ lb. minced mussel or oyster meats
½ t. ground pepper
2 t. celery seed (or lovage)
1 t. cumin
⅛ t. fennel
1 raw egg
1 c. bread crumbs
casings; 2 T. olive oil

In a mortar, grind together pepper, celery seed (or lovage), cumin, and fennel. Mix with the minced shellfish meats. Bind with well beaten egg and bread crumbs. Stuff this mixture into sausage casings and sauté over low heat for 20 minutes in olive oil, in a covered pan.

*A really splendid first course can be made by slicing the mussel sausage into an apple pie with a sprinkle of cinnamon. Bake, and serve when cooled.*

### Prawn or Lobster Forcemeats

½ lb. minced prawn or lobster meats
½ t. pepper
2 T. fish-pickle (see p. 2)
1 raw egg; 1 c. bread crumbs
casings; 2 T. olive oil

Season prawn or lobster forcemeats with the pepper and fish-pickle. Bind with well beaten egg and bread crumbs. Stuff into sausage casings and sauté over low heat in olive oil for 20 minutes in a covered pan.

*Serve hot with steamed rice or, on a warm summer day, chilled and sliced into a simple lettuce salad.*

### Spiced Pork Liver Sausage

¼ lb. pork (or beef) liver
2 T. olive oil
½ t. pepper
½ t. rosemary (or rue)
3 cloves or 6 juniper berries
casings
1 raw egg
1 c. bread crumbs

Remove membranes from liver, slice thinly, and sauté in olive oil for 3–4 minutes on each side, then chop finely.

In a mortar, grind together coriander, pepper, rosemary, and juniper berries or cloves. Add the seasonings to the liver forcemeat, and bind with well beaten egg and bread crumbs. Stuff the mixture into sausage casings, and sauté over low heat in olive oil for 20 minutes, in a covered pan.

*Don't be squeamish about calf's brains. Their flavor is more subtle than most meats and wonderful when spiced.*

## Calf's Brains and Egg Dumplings

*1 lb. calf's brains*
*½ t. pepper*
*1½ t. celery seed (or lovage)*
*1 t. oregano*
*5 raw eggs*

In a mortar, grind the pepper, celery seed (or lovage), and oregano. Add to chopped, cooked calf's brains, and combine with well beaten eggs. Empty the mixture into a baking pan, and cook in a 325° F oven for 30 minutes. Remove from heat and cut into cubes.

*Sauce:*
*½ t. pepper*
*1 t. celery seed (or lovage)*
*½ t. oregano*
*1 c. meat stock; flour*

For the sauce, grind together pepper, celery seed (or lovage), and oregano. Add to stock, bring to a boil, then simmer and thicken with flour. Reheat the brain dumplings in this thick sauce, and serve with a sprinkling of pepper.

## Shellfish Forcemeats or Sausage

*¼ lb. minced shellfish meats*
*½ t. ground pepper*
*1 t. celery seed (or lovage)*
*¼ c. grated almonds or pine nuts*
*1 raw egg*
*1 c. bread crumbs*
*casings; 2 T. olive oil*
*wine sauce (see p. 3)*

In a mortar, grind together pepper and celery seed (or lovage). Mix with the shellfish meats and nuts. Bind with well beaten egg and bread crumbs. Then stuff into sausage casings, and sauté gently in olive oil in a covered pan for 20 minutes.

When cooked and lightly browned, season with wine sauce, and serve.

## *Pepper (Myrtle) Sausages*

*½ lb. choice pork*
*1 c. fresh bread*
*¼ c. wine*
*½ t. ground pepper*
*a few peppercorns (or myrtle berries, if available)*
*(meat stock)*
*½ c. almonds or pine nuts*
*¼ c. boiled wine; casings*

Finely grind pork, and then pound it in a mortar with bread moistened with wine. Add pepper and roughly ground peppercorns (or crushed myrtle berries), and stock, if too dry. Mix with finely chopped nuts. Stuff into casings, or form into balls and wrap in casings. Sauté in boiled wine.

*Myrtle berries, once common in Western cookery, were superseded by the peppercorn during the reign of Augustus Caesar. Among Apicius' recipes their presence is an archaism. Fry with potatoes and serve with peas for supper, or with range eggs for a savory holiday breakfast.*

## FISH–PICKLE AND WATER SAUCE, APOTHERMUM, AND THICK SAUCE

ISICIA PLENA *Pheasant Forcemeats* Take the fat of freshly killed pheasants, brown and slice into cubes. [Mix these] with pepper, stock, and boiled wine. Shape each one into a dumpling. Poach in fish-pickle mixed with water and serve.

HYDROGARATA ISICIA SIC FACIES *Forcemeats with Fish-pickle and Water* Grind pepper, lovage, a very small amount of pellitory, and pour a little stock [over these seasonings]. Add cistern water and empty into a saucepan. Add the forcemeats and place the pan on the heat of the fire to cook. Serve. To be eaten just as it is.

IN ISICIATO PULLO *For Chicken Forcemeats* Make with 1 pound of the best oil, ¼ pint of stock, and ½ ounce of pepper.

ALITER DE PULLO *For Chicken* Grind thirty-one peppercorns, put in a cup of the best quality stock, as much of boiled wine, and eleven cups of water. Put it on the heat to cook.

ISICIUM SIMPLEX *Plain Forcemeats* Mix a quarter cup of fish-pickle with one and three-quarter cups of water, some green celery, and a spoonful of ground pepper. Cook the forcemeat dumplings [in this mixture]. This recipe will promote regularity. The lees of spiced wine can be added to the fish-pickle and water.

[UNTITLED] [*Forcemeats*] Peacock forcemeats are the best if the hard skin is first fried and so softened. Pheasants are the second choice, rabbits come third, chickens fourth, and the flesh of tender piglets, fifth.

ISICIA AMULATA A BALINEO SIC FACIES *Forcemeats with Starch from a Vat* Grind pepper, lovage, oregano, a small quantity of silphium, and the least ginger. Mix with measures of a little honey and stock, and pour over the forcemeats. Bring to the boil, and then thicken the gravy with starch. Serve it to be sipped.

## *Seasoned Chicken Forcemeat Dumplings*

*¹/₂ lb. cooked chicken or pheasant meats, chopped*
*³/₄ t. ground pepper*
*1 T. boiled white wine*
*1 raw egg*
*chicken stock*
*water*
*1 T. fish-pickle (see p. 2)*

Take cooked, browned meat and dice into small cubes. Season with the pepper and boiled wine. Add well beaten egg and just enough stock to bind. Shape into balls and poach gently for 30 minutes, or until done, in water seasoned with fish-pickle.

*The fish-pickle adds a deliciously exotic touch.*

## *Meat Dumplings Cooked in Fish-pickle Sauce*

*¹/₂ lb. uncooked forcemeats (see Seasoned Chicken Forcemeats above)*
*Sauce:*
*¹/₂ t. ground pepper*
*¹/₂ t. celery seed (or lovage)*
*pinch of chamomile (or pellitory)*
*1 T. fish-pickle (see p. 2)*
*1 c. water*

In a mortar, grind pepper, celery seed (or lovage), and a dash of chamomile (or pellitory). Add fish-pickle, and blend with water. Mix and pour into a pan. Poach the dumplings in this sauce, adding a little more water if necessary. Serve when the liquid has been evaporated by the heat.

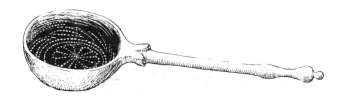

## Roman Chicken Broth

*1 stewing chicken*
*10 peppercorns*
*½ c. reduced vegetable stock*
*½ c. boiled white wine*
*water*

In a mortar, grind peppercorns. Mix with reduced stock, boiled white wine, and water to cover. Add the chicken cut in pieces, and cook gently over low heat until the fowl is done.

*Remove the chicken pieces and what remains is a classic cure for the common cold.*

## Simple Seafood Dumplings

*½ lb. mussel forcemeats (see p. 8)*
*1 T. fish-pickle (see p. 2)*
*1 c. water*
*½ c. finely chopped celery*
*1 t. ground pepper*
*spiced wine sediments*

Mix fish-pickle with water, chopped celery, and pepper. Bring to a boil, then simmer over very low heat. Add seafood dumplings to the mixture and cook till done.

*If you have any leftover* Spiced Wine Apicius, *the sediments can be added while cooking for a richer flavor.*

## Seafood Forcemeats with Gingered Gravy

*½ lb. mussel forcemeats (see p. 8)*
*½ t. ground pepper*
*1 t. celery seed (or lovage)*
*1 t. oregano*
*¼ t. ginger*
*1 t. honey*
*1½ c. shellfish stock*
*flour*

In a mortar, grind pepper, celery seed (or lovage), oregano, and ginger. Combine with honey and stock. Pour into a pan and add the seafood forcemeats. Cover and cook over very low heat until done. Thicken the gravy with flour, and serve.

*This sauce is equally delicious served with shrimps or other shellfish instead of Apicius' mussel forcemeats.*

### *Thick Sauce for Meat Dumplings*

*2 c. chicken broth*
*1 T. chives*
*pinch of aniseed*
*½ t. ground pepper*
*1 t. celery seed*
*¼ c. sweet white wine or muscatel*
*flour*

Pour broth into a saucepan with chives and aniseed. Bring to a boil, then gently simmer for 25 minutes. Add ground pepper, celery seed, and wine. Stir in flour, to thicken, and serve.

*This sauce is also very good when used to "dress up" meatballs or hamburgers.*

### *Pork Almond Sausage with Leeks*

*1 lb. finely ground pork*
*½ t. ground pepper*
*1 t. cumin*
*pinch of rosemary*
*1 c. bread crumbs*
*½ c. almonds, grated*
*1 raw egg*
*casings*
*1 c. pork or vegetable stock*
*leeks*
*aniseed*

In a mortar, grind together pepper, cumin, and rosemary. Add to bread crumbs, and almonds, and mix with the pork. Bind with well beaten egg and moisten as needed with stock. Stuff into sausage casings, then poach the sausages in equal parts of water and stock for 30 minutes.

Serve with leeks cooked in water seasoned with aniseed.

*These and the subsequent sausages are meals in themselves, delicious with potatoes and green vegetables, and taken with cold lager beer. However, the ultimate dish is achieved when* Pork Almond, Lucanian, *or* Pork, Barley and Bacon Sausages *are sliced into the stuffing ingredients for a roast lamb or kid, almost—but not quite—too much.*

## Small Black Pork Pudding

6 hard-boiled egg yolks
¼ c. almonds, grated
1 chopped onion
½ c. thinly sliced leeks
blood
½ lb. ground pork or beef
1 raw egg
½ c. bread crumbs
½ t. pepper
casings
1 c. meat or vegetable stock
½ c. red wine

Mix the chopped yolks of hard-boiled eggs, nuts, onion, leeks, and sufficient blood to moisten. Combine with ground beef or pork. Season with pepper and bind with well beaten egg and bread crumbs. Then stuff all into sausage casings. Put stock and red wine in a pan with the sausages, cover, bring to a boil, then cook over low heat for 30 minutes.

*As an Englishman, I enjoy Black Pudding at breakfast with fried eggs and tomatoes—the stuff upon which Empires were built.*

## Lucanian Spiced Sausage

½ t. pepper
½ t. cumin
1 t. savory
1 T. parsley
pinch of rosemary (or rue)
6 cloves or juniper berries (or laurel berries)
1 lb. finely ground beef or pork
¼ c. almonds, grated
1 c. bread crumbs
¼ c. beef stock
1 raw egg
casings
2 T. olive oil

In a mortar, grind together pepper, cumin, savory, parsley, rosemary (or rue), and cloves or juniper berries. Combine with meat, and add nuts and bread crumbs. Moisten with stock, and bind with well beaten egg. Stuff into sausage casing, and sauté in olive oil in a covered pan, over low heat for 30 minutes.

*This is a delicious savory sausage either on its own, or as a meal with green vegetables and boiled potatoes. It is also used as an ingredient in other recipes.*

## Calf's Brain and Almond Sausage

*1 lb. cooked calf's or pork brains*
*¼ c. almonds, grated*
*1 t. pepper*
*½ t. ginger*
*1 c. bread crumbs*
*1 c. beef or pork stock*
*1 raw egg*
*casings*

Finely chop the brains and mix with grated almonds. Season with pepper and ginger. Add bread crumbs, and stock to moisten. Bind with well beaten egg and stuff into sausage casings. Cook in a little water, over low heat, in a covered pan for 20 minutes. Then brown in the oven and serve.

*A delicious combination of flavors which work equally well without the casing.*

## Pork, Barley, and Bacon Sausage

*1 lb. ground pork*
*½ c. cooked pearl barley (or*
*1 c. bread crumbs)*
*2 leeks, finely chopped*
*½ c. cooked bacon, chopped*
*¼ c. almonds, grated*
*1 t. pepper*
*2 t. celery seed (or lovage)*
*pork or beef stock*
*1 raw egg*
*casings*

Mix cooked barley or bread crumbs with leeks, bacon, almonds, and meat. Season with pepper, celery seed (or lovage). Moisten with stock as needed, and bind with well beaten egg. Stuff into sausage casings.

Cook in a little water, in a covered pan, for 30 minutes, then brown in the oven.

*This and the other sausages may also be served cold, in slices, as snacks or on picnics. A bottle of German or Czechoslovakian lager will go down very well at the same time.*

## Sausage in a Ring with Thick Wine Sauce

*1 lb. Lucanian Spiced Sausage meat (see p. 15)*
*casing*
*2 T. olive oil*
*1 c. wine sauce (see p. 3)*
*flour*

Prepare the sausage meat and stuff into a 1 foot sausage casing. Tie in a circle and sauté in a hot frying pan with olive oil. Cover and cook over low heat for 30 minutes.

Serve in hot wine sauce thickened with flour.

*The ring of sausage can be placed on top of a roast lamb or kid, perhaps with a coronet of myrtle or laurel leaves, to evoke cheers from your dinner guests.*

# The Gardener

### Beets with Leeks in Wine

½ lb. young whole beets
3 thinly sliced leeks
½ t. ground pepper
½ t. cumin
1 c. beet stock
½ c. sweet raisin wine or muscatel

Cook beets, drain, reserve liquid, and slice. Put them in a saucepan with leeks. In a mortar, grind pepper and cumin. Add to the leeks and beets. Then add stock and sweet wine. Pour this sauce over the vegetables, bring to a boil, then simmer till leeks are cooked.

*The lovely deep color of this dish adds beauty to your table. Serve with chicken or game birds, with brown or wild rice.*

### Fern Roots and Beets with Almonds

3–4 medium sized beets
water
¼ c. boiled red wine
¼ t. pepper
¼ t. cumin
2 T. olive oil
¼ c. almonds, finely chopped
1 c. roasted polypody, deer fern, lady fern, or bracken fern roots
½ c. beet stock

Put beets in a saucepan, cover with water, and cook until tender. Drain, reserve liquid, slice, and sauté lightly in a mixture of boiled wine, pepper, cumin, and olive oil.

Meanwhile, combine chopped almonds and chopped fern root with stock. Pour this over the sautéed beets, cover, reheat, and remove from heat.

## Varro's Recipe for Beets with Chicken

*10 small beets*
*¼ c. mead, or sweet white wine*
*1 T. olive oil*
*½ lb. part cooked chicken pieces*

Put whole, small beets, into a saucepan. Add mead or sweet wine, olive oil, and enough water to cover. Bring to a boil, add chicken pieces, and cook till done.

*A very good combination. Be prepared, though, for beet colored meats.*

## Leeks with Celery

*1 bunch fresh celery*
*4 leeks*

*Sauce:*
*½ t. ground pepper*
*¼ c. vegetable stock*
*2 c. celery stock*
*1 t. honey*

Put pieces of celery in water, bring to a boil, then simmer for 15 minutes. Drain and reserve celery stock. In a fresh saucepan, cook the heads and tender parts of leeks until ⅓ of the water has boiled away.

For the sauce, combine pepper, stock, and honey, and add to strained celery stock. Bring to a boil and simmer for 25 minutes to reduce. Put the cooked leeks into a new saucepan and pour the sauce over them. Heat the sauce with the leeks and serve.

The celery stalks may be added, if you wish.

## Squash with Herbs and Spices

*1 medium sized squash, zucchini, or pumpkin*

*Sauce:*
*½ t. ground pepper*
*¼ t. cumin*
*¼ t. ginger*
*pinch of rosemary (or rue)*
*1 t. cider vinegar*
*2 T. boiled red wine*
*½ c. squash stock*

Peel and cut the squash, gourd, or pumpkin, into pieces, put in a pan with water, and cook till done. Press the water out of the cooked squash, and reserve liquid. Put the squash into a fresh pan.

For the sauce, in a mortar, grind together pepper, cumin, ginger, and rosemary (or rue). Add vinegar, wine, and stock. Pour this sauce over the squash and simmer till well cooked.

Serve with a sprinkling of pepper.

## GOURDS

❡ Apicius used the word "cucurbita" for this division of his recipes for garden vegetables and, indeed, many fruits of the order cucurbitaceae are delicious when prepared classically. This would include gourd, pumpkin, squash, zucchini, or vegetable marrow.

GUSTUM DE CUCURBITIS *Gourd Antepast* Squeeze out the water from the cooked gourds and put them into a shallow pan. In a mortar, add pepper, cumin, a little silphium, that is laser root, a little rue, and blend with stock and vinegar. Put in a little boiled wine for color. Pour the sauce into the pan. When [the gourd antepast is] boiled a second and third time, remove [from the heat] and sprinkle over it a very small quantity of pepper.

ALITER CUCURBITAS IURE COLOCASIORUM *Gourds in Broad Bean Broth* Cook the gourds in water as you would broad beans. [Meanwhile] mix pepper, cumin, rue, and sprinkle with vinegar and stock. Simmer in a pan. Add to this a little olive oil. Put into the pan the chopped and drained gourds. Heat. Thicken with starch, sprinkle with pepper, and serve.

CUCURBITAS MORE ALEXANDRINO *Gourds Alexandrine* Boil the gourds and squeeze them [to extract the water]. Sprinkle them with salt and put them in a saucepan. Now grind pepper, cumin, coriander seed, fresh mint, and laser root. Pour vinegar over [these seasonings]. Then toss in some dates and nuts, and grind. Blend with honey, vinegar, stock, boiled wine, and olive oil. Pour this over the gourds. When [the dish] has been brought to the boil, sprinkle with pepper and serve.

❡ This recipe, named after Alexandria, in Egypt, is evidence of the influence of Egyptian cooking upon *The Roman Cookery of Apicius.*

ALITER CUCURBITAS ELIXATAS *Stewed Gourds* [Cook] in stock, oil, and unmixed wine.

## Squash in Bean Broth with Rosemary Sauce

*1 medium squash, gourd,*
*zucchini, or pumpkin*
*bean stock*

Take a whole squash and steam it in bean broth. When done, slice open the cooked squash, cut out the flesh, and press out moisture.

*Sauce:*
*½ t. ground pepper*
*¼ t. cumin*
*pinch of rosemary (or rue)*
*1 t. cider vinegar*
*1 c. gourd or vegetable stock*
*1 T. olive oil or butter*
*flour*

Meanwhile, in a mortar, grind together pepper, cumin, and rosemary (or rue). Add to vinegar and stock. Heat this sauce in a pan with butter or olive oil. Add the cooked squash to the sauce, and simmer for 10 minutes over low heat. Thicken with flour, and serve with a sprinkling of pepper.

## Alexandrine Squash

*1 medium squash, gourd,*
*zucchini, or pumpkin*
*water*

Cut squash in pieces, and steam in water till cooked. Press the water out of the cooked flesh, and put into a cooking pot.

*Sauce:*
*½ t. ground pepper*
*¼ t. cumin*
*½ t. coriander*
*½ t. mint*
*¼ t. ginger*
*1 t. cider vinegar*
*¼ c. dates, finely chopped*
*¼ c. almonds, finely chopped*
*1 t. honey*
*¼ c. boiled white wine*
*½ c. squash or vegetable stock*
*1 T. olive oil or butter*

For the sauce, in a mortar, grind pepper, cumin, coriander, mint, and ginger. Combine with vinegar, chopped dates and almonds, honey, boiled wine, stock, and olive oil or butter. Pour this sauce over the squash, bring gently to a boil, and simmer briefly to blend flavors. Sprinkle with pepper, and serve.

*Squash is a versatile and appealing vegetable. It marries well with almost every meat dish, and adds a dash of unexpected color. This particular recipe from* The Roman Cookery of Apicius *always draws applause.*

## Squash Cooked in Wine

*1 medium squash, gourd,*
*zucchini, or pumpkin*
*½ c. squash or vegetable stock*
*1 T. olive oil or butter*
*¼ c. white wine*

Peel and slice the zucchini, squash, or gourd. Put the slices into a shallow pan, and add stock, olive oil or butter, and white wine. Cover, bring to a boil, and simmer gently until done.

*Serve with a sprinkling of pepper as a side dish with fish poached in a Roman sauce.*

## Squash in Oregano Wine Sauce

*1 medium squash, gourd,*
*zucchini, or pumpkin*
*1 c. wine sauce (see p. 3)*
*1 t. celery seed (or lovage)*
*1 t. oregano*
*¼ t. cumin*
*ground pepper*

Gently simmer the sliced squash in wine sauce seasoned with celery seed (or lovage), oregano, and cumin. When cooked, serve the squash in the sauce, with pepper, to taste.

*Especially delicious served with venison steak, or any other red meat.*

## Steamed Squash Sautéed with Cumin

*1 medium squash, gourd,*
*zucchini, or pumpkin*
*water*
*1 T. olive oil or butter*
*¼ t. cumin*
*ground pepper*

Peel and slice the squash, gourd, or zucchini, and steam with water until tender. Drain and put into a hot frying pan greased with olive oil or butter. Season with cumin. Sauté lightly, and serve with a sprinkling of pepper.

*Very good with slices of* Roast Pork Apicius.

## Sautéed Squash in Herb Sauce

*1 medium onion, thinly sliced*
*1 T. olive oil*
*¼ t. ground pepper*
*¼ t. celery seed (or lovage)*
*¼ t. oregano*
*dash of cumin*
*3 c. diced squash or gourds*
*½ c. squash or vegetable stock*
*¼ c. white wine*
*1 t. olive oil*
*(flour)*

Sauté sliced onion in olive oil. In a mortar, grind pepper, celery seed (or lovage), and oregano. Add to onions, with a dash of cumin. Stir. Then add diced squash. Add stock, white wine, and olive oil. Stir repeatedly over medium heat until the gourds are cooked. If you wish, thicken the liquid with flour, and serve.

## Spiced Squash with Chicken and Apricots

*4 c. diced squash or gourd*
*3–4 lb. chicken*
*green olives*
*1 c. apricots, fresh or dried*
*mushrooms (or truffles), sliced*
*3 celery stalks, chopped*
*1 t. ground pepper*
*pinch of caraway seeds*
*¼ t. cumin*
*½ t. ginger*
*1 t. mint*
*½ t. coriander*
*¼ c. dates, finely chopped*
*1 T. honey*
*½ c. white wine*
*½ c. vegetable or chicken stock*
*1 T. olive oil or butter*
*1 t. white wine vinegar or cider vinegar*

Put diced squash and a whole chicken stuffed with olives into a large cooking pot. To the pot add apricots, sliced mushrooms (or peeled truffles), and celery.

In a mortar, grind pepper, caraway, cumin, ginger, mint, and coriander. Combine with dates, honey, white wine, stock, olive oil or butter, and vinegar. Stir these ingredients to mix flavors and add to the pot. Cover, and cook slowly over low heat until the chicken is done.

*This is a splendid main course with which to introduce your guests to festive Roman cookery. Precede with* Spiced Pork Hors d'oeuvres *and a spinach and celery salad.* Salubrissime!

*A whole new dimension opens up for using cucumbers, if they are cooked as in these Roman recipes.*

## Cucumbers Cooked with Wine Sauce

Peel and thickly slice the cucumbers. Cover with stock or wine sauce (see p. 3). Bring to a boil, then simmer gently till cooked.

## Cucumbers with Calf's Brains

*4 cucumbers, sliced*
*1 c. cooked calf's brains, chopped*
*1 c. veal stock*
*¼ t. cumin*
*1 t. honey*
*½ t. celery seed*
*2 t. olive oil*
*2 raw egg yolks*
*ground pepper*

Slice the cucumbers. Put into a cooking pot with calf's brains, veal stock, cumin, honey, celery seed, and olive oil. Bring to a boil, then simmer till cucumbers are lightly cooked. Bind with well beaten yolks, and serve with a sprinkling of pepper.

## Cooked Cucumbers with Fennel

*4 cucumbers, sliced*
*½ t. ground pepper*
*½ t. mint (or pennyroyal)*
*1 T. honey, or 2 T. sweet raisin wine*
*½ c. veal or chicken stock*
*1 t. white wine vinegar*
*fennel*

Slice the cucumbers into a pot. Season with pepper, mint (or pennyroyal), and honey or raisin wine. Add stock and vinegar. Bring to a boil, then cover, and simmer gently. Sprinkle with fennel to taste, and serve when cucumbers are lightly cooked.

## Pumpkin with Squash or Apples

*3 c. diced pumpkin and squash, or apples*
*butter*

Peel and dice the pumpkin and squash, and arrange in a buttered baking dish.

*Sauce:*
*¼ t. pepper*
*pinch of mint (or pennyroyal)*
*1 T. honey, or 2 T. sweet raisin wine*
*¼ c. squash or vegetable stock*
*dash of white wine vinegar*
*1 t. ginger*

For the sauce, mix pepper, mint (or pennyroyal), honey or raisin wine, stock, and vinegar. Pour the sauce over the pumpkin. Bake in a 325°F oven for 30 minutes or until tender. Sprinkle with ginger as the dish is cooking.

*Serve with chicken, duck, or pork entrées, for an outstanding combination.*

The recipes which follow are adapted to be used for all brassicas and other greens.

## Cauliflower or Broccoli in Celery Mint Sauce

*1 cauliflower, cabbage, or bunch of broccoli*

Take cauliflower, cabbage, or broccoli, quarter them, and put in a saucepan.

*Sauce:*
*¼ t. cumin*
*2 T. white wine*
*1 T. olive oil*

For the first sauce, combine the cumin, wine, olive oil, and enough water to steam the vegetables. Add to the vegetables, bring to a boil, then simmer gently till done.

*Sauce:*
*¼ t. ground pepper*
*½ t. celery seed (or lovage)*
*½ t. mint*
*pinch of rosemary (or rue)*
*¼ t. coriander*
*½ c. vegetable stock*
*2 T. white wine vinegar*
*1 T. olive oil or butter*

Meanwhile, in a mortar, grind pepper, celery seed (or lovage), mint, rosemary (or rue) and coriander. Add to stock, vinegar, and olive oil or butter. Bring to a boil, then simmer to reduce for 25 minutes. Serve over the cooked, strained vegetables.

(All three vegetables may be combined in this recipe).

## Broccoli and Cabbage in Coriander Wine Sauce

*1 bunch of broccoli heads, or the tender leaves of a cabbage, parboiled*

Take pre-cooked broccoli heads or cabbage leaves and simmer in the following sauce.

*Sauce:*
*½ t. coriander*
*1 medium onion, sliced*
*pinch of cumin*
*¼ t. ground pepper*
*¼ c. sweet raisin wine, or boiled white wine*
*2 T. olive oil*

For the sauce, combine the coriander, onion rings, cumin, pepper, raisin wine or boiled wine, and olive oil or butter. Bring to a boil, then add vegetables, and simmer together gently for 10 minutes to combine flavors.

## Spiced Broccoli, Cabbage, and Brussel Sprouts

*1 bunch broccoli heads*
*½ medium cabbage*
*½ lb. brussel sprouts*
*¼ c. vegetable stock*
*2 T. olive oil*
*2 T. white wine*
*cumin*
*½ t. ground pepper*
*1 T. chives*
*1 t. roasted coriander seeds*

Chop the cabbage into wedges and steam in water with the other vegetables. Drain, and reserve liquid. Put vegetables into a saucepan and simmer till tender in a mixture of the stock, olive oil, wine, and cumin to taste. Before serving, garnish with pepper, chives, and roasted coriander seeds.

*This exciting sauce wakes up the greens, and goes very well with a poached white fish.*

## Chestnut Sauce for Greens

*2 T. butter*
*2 T. white pastry flour*
*1 c. milk*
*¼ c. dark raisins*
*¼ c. roasted chestnuts or almonds, chopped*
*ground pepper*

Over low heat, first melt butter and mix with flour. Stir in milk and cook gently. Add raisins and chopped roasted chestnuts, or almonds. Simmer to blend flavors, then pour over the greens. Sprinkle with pepper and serve.

*A colorful, nutty sauce that I use as a complement to meats which have been cooked with little or no seasoning. Sometimes it is effective to simply season one dish in your menu in a Roman manner, in order to vary the mood of a meal.*

## Leeks with White Wine

*2 leeks, sliced*
*1 T. olive oil*
*water*

Cut leeks into 1 inch slices. Put in pot with olive oil. Add a little water, bring to a boil, and simmer until the leeks are tender. Drain.

*Sauce:*
*1 t. olive oil*
*¼ c. chicken stock*
*¼ c. white wine*

For the sauce, mix olive oil and stock. Add white wine. Heat and simmer gently for 15 minutes to reduce. Pour over the cooked leeks, and serve.

*Delicious with many meat and seafood dishes.*

## Beets and Leeks in Raisin Sauce

½ lb. young whole beets
3 or 4 sliced leeks
1 t. coriander
¼ t. cumin
¼ c. raisins
2 c. vegetable stock
flour
olive oil
white wine vinegar or
cider vinegar

In a mortar, grind together coriander and cumin. Add to raisins and stock. Bring to a boil, then add the beets and leeks. Simmer gently for 25 minutes to reduce the liquid or till vegetables are tender. Thicken with flour, and serve the vegetables in the sauce with a sprinkling of olive oil and vinegar.

*These ingredients do wonders for the familiar beet.*

## Pickled Beets

3–4 medium beets
2 T. mustard seed
water
1 c. white wine vinegar
1 c. unchlorinated water

Put whole beets into a saucepan and cover with water. Add mustard seed. Cook until the beets can be pricked easily with a fork. Drain and slice the beets into pint jars. Add mustard seed to each jar. In a saucepan, mix vinegar with water. Heat and then pour over the sliced beets. Seal. Yields two pints of pickled beets. Serve in oil and vinegar dressing.

½ c. olive oil
2 T. white wine vinegar

Alternatively, cook the beets as above and slice them into a bowl. Add olive oil and vinegar. Stir well. Chill and serve. Use only tender beets.

## Green Chervil Sauce

¼ t. coriander
1 T. chopped onion
2 sprigs fresh chervil, finely chopped
1 sprig lovage or celery leaves, finely chopped
1 fresh mint leaf
½ c. white wine
½ c. vegetable or chicken stock
1 t. white wine vinegar
1 t. honey
flour

In a saucepan, combine coriander and onion with fresh, chopped herbs. Combine with wine, stock, vinegar, and honey. Gently bring to a boil, then simmer over low heat for 10 minutes. Thicken with flour, and serve with fish, meat, or with cabbage rolls.

*Care must be taken to assert the chervil's subtle flavor in the face of the other seasonings. This is a very fine sauce used with poached or baked fish. You may wish to reduce the quantity of lovage if this beautiful herb is new to your cuisine. Lovage can also be strewn decoratively atop the fish, like a coronet of parsley.*

## Turnips in Cumin Sauce

1 lb. turnips, cubed
water

Peel turnips, and cut into cubes. Steam in a little water till half-cooked, drain, and reserve liquid.

Sauce:
½ t. cumin
pinch of rosemary (or rue)
¼ t. ginger
1 t. honey
2 t. olive oil
¼ c. boiled white wine
1 c. turnip stock
flour
pepper

For the sauce, mix cumin, rosemary (or rue), ginger, honey, olive oil, boiled wine, and sufficient stock to cover. Add to the turnips and finish cooking them in the sauce. Thicken with flour, and serve with a sprinkling of pepper.

*From my mother I inherited the delightful English habit of cooking together equal portions of turnips and carrots, which works very well here. If possible, sprinkle with "white" pepper.*

## Pureed Greens in Lovage-Savory Sauce

*½ large cabbage, sliced*
*1 c. cauliflower, or 2 c. greens*
*water*

Use tender young cabbage, or cauliflower, (or broccoli, brussel sprouts, or other early greens). Simmer them in a little water, drain, press, and chop very finely.

*Sauce:*
*½ t. pepper*
*2 t. celery seed (or 1 T. fresh lovage)*
*½ t. savory*
*2 T. chopped onion*
*½ c. vegetable stock*
*flour*
*1 t. olive oil or butter*
*¼ c. white wine*

For the sauce, blend the pepper, celery seed (or lovage), savory, onion, stock, olive oil or butter, and white wine. Bring to a boil, thicken with flour, and serve with pureed greens.

*Though the Romans favored purees, perhaps because of dental problems, today these sauces are just as delicious over steamed, slightly crisp vegetables.*

## Pureed Celery in Lovage-Oregano Sauce

*2 c. chopped celery*

Place chopped celery in a pan, and simmer in water till tender. Drain, and press out the moisture from the vegetable.

*Sauce:*
*¼ t. ground pepper*
*½ t. celery seed (or lovage)*
*½ t. oregano*
*2 t. chopped onion*
*¼ c. white wine*
*½ c. vegetable stock*
*1 t. olive oil*
*flour*

For the sauce, grind together in a mortar, pepper, celery seed (or lovage), and oregano. Add to onion, white wine, stock, and olive oil, and heat. Finish cooking the celery in the sauce and thicken with flour. Serve with a sprinkling of pepper.

*There are a number of different kinds of nettles. There are wild nettles which they call female, and also cultivated nettles. . . . Indeed, the young female nettles are not disagreeable to the taste when they are picked in the spring, and they are eaten faithfully by many people to drive away diseases during the whole year to come. And the root of the wild nettle will make any kind of meat more tender when it is boiled with it.*

                                                      Pliny.

## ENDIVE AND LETTUCES*

[UNTITLED]  [*Endive*]  Endive is served with [a dressing of] fish-pickle, a little oil, and chopped onion. Endive may be used in place of lettuce in winter, in a dressing or [with] honey and sharp vinegar.

*Endive is good whether raw or cooked for both the healthy and the infirm, but raw endive is best eaten after drying for a day in the sun.*

                                          Anthimus.

[UNTITLED]  [*Lettuce*]  Serve lettuce in [a dressing of] "oxyporum," vinegar, and a little fish-pickle.

AD DIGESTIONEM ET INFLATIONEM ET NE LACTUCAE LAEDANT  *An Aid to Digestion and a Preventative of Flatulence So That Lettuce Will Not Harm You*  Two ounces of cumin, one ounce of ginger, one ounce of green rue, twelve scruples of plump dates, one ounce of pepper, nine ounces of honey. The cumin should be either Ethiopian or Syrian or Libyan. Grind the cumin and then pour it into vinegar. [Strain and] when it has dried, combine all the ingredients with the honey. When necessary, mix half a spoonful with vinegar and fish-pickle and take half a spoonful after dinner.

   ❡ The point of this recipe seems to be to arm the stomach for the onslaught of a rich Apician banquet, rather than enjoyment of the lettuce salad.

---

*Eaten at the "gustatio," the light first course which began a formal Roman meal.

## Onion and Lettuce Puree in Lovage Mint Sauce

*1 head of lettuce*
*1 onion*
*water*

Place the vegetables in a pan with a little water and steam till tender. Drain, press, and chop very finely.

*Sauce:*
*¼ t. ground pepper*
*1 T. lovage (or celery seed)*
*½ t. celery seed*
*sprig of mint, chopped*
*1 c. chicken stock*
*1 t. olive oil*
*dash of white wine vinegar or cider vinegar*

For the sauce, in a mortar, grind the pepper, lovage (or celery seed), and celery seed. Add to mint, stock, olive oil, and vinegar. Bring to a boil, then simmer for 25 minutes to reduce. Pour over the vegetable puree and serve.

## Watercress Salad

*watercress*
*1 T. fish-pickle (see p. 2)*
*3 T. olive oil*
*1 T. cider vinegar*
*water*
*¼ t. ground pepper*
*pinch of cumin*
*2 T. pistachio nuts, chopped*

Use fresh watercress and serve it as a salad in a dressing made by combining the fish-pickle, olive oil, and vinegar.

Alternatively, put the watercress in a pan with a little water, season with pepper, cumin, and chopped pistachio nuts, and simmer gently for 2–3 minutes over low heat.

## Endive in Dressing

*endive*
*1 t. fish-pickle (see p. 2)*
*3 T. olive oil*
*1 T. onion, finely chopped*
*1 t. white wine vinegar*
*1 t. honey*
*3 T. olive oil*
*1 T. cider vinegar*

Serve endive in a dressing made from fish-pickle, olive oil, chopped onion, and vinegar.

Or serve in a dressing of honey, vinegar, and olive oil.

*Once discovered, the rich flavoring of fish-pickle is likely to become a favorite condiment or ingredient.*

*The first two recipes below are dressings in which the boiled artichoke leaves are dipped and eaten. The last is a sauce in which the artichokes are boiled whole. After cooking in this manner, a dressing may be added according to taste.*

## Artichokes with Fish-pickle Dressing

*3–4 artichokes*
*water*
*1 t. fish-pickle (see p. 2)*
*½ c. olive oil*
*3 hard-boiled eggs, very finely chopped*

Cut off the artichoke stems, remove the tough bottom leaves and trim ½ inch from the tips of the remaining ones. Put in a covered pan with water, and steam for 45 minutes, or until tender. Chill.

For the dressing, combine fish-pickle, olive oil, and chopped egg. Serve cold with the chilled artichokes.

## Artichokes with Hot Herb Dressing

*3–4 artichokes*
*pinch of rosemary (or rue)*
*2 fresh mint leaves (or 1 t. dried)*
*¼ t. coriander*
*pinch of fennel*
*¼ t. ground pepper*
*½ t. celery seed (or lovage)*
*2 t. olive oil*
*1 c. vegetable stock or water*
*(2 t. honey)*

Trim and steam the artichokes as in preceding recipe.

For the dressing, grind together rosemary (or rue), mint, coriander, fennel, pepper, and celery seed (or lovage). Add to olive oil and stock. (To make a sweet dressing, add honey.) Bring to a boil, then simmer gently for 10 minutes to blend flavors. Serve with the steamed artichokes.

## Cumin Spiced Artichokes

*3–4 artichokes*
*1 c. vegetable stock*
*½ t. pepper*
*1 t. cumin*
*2 t. olive oil*

Steam artichokes in a covered pan in stock seasoned with pepper, cumin, and olive oil.

*Cumin brings a very pleasant "new" flavor to the familiar artichoke.*

## Coriander Parsnips Cooked in Wine

*6 whole parsnips*
*1 c. water*
*2 t. olive oil*
*¼ c. white wine*
*1 ½ t. coriander*
*a few peppercorns*
*2 t. olive oil or butter*

Put cleaned parsnips in a pan. Add water seasoned with olive oil, white wine, coriander, and peppercorns. Bring to a boil, then simmer gently for 10 minutes or until parsnips are tender. Drain and serve with olive oil or butter.

*This and the following recipes show a wonderful variation of flavors for the humble parsnip.*

## Celery Seed Sauce for Parsnips

*6 cooked parsnips, sliced*
*water*
*1 t. celery seed*
*pinch of rosemary (or rue)*
*½ t. ground pepper*
*1 t. honey*
*¼ c. white wine*
*1 c. vegetable stock*
*2 t. olive oil or butter*
*flour*
*ground pepper*

To make the sauce, first grind celery seed, rosemary (or rue), and pepper together in a mortar. Blend with honey, white wine, stock, and olive oil or butter. Simmer for 10 minutes, and thicken with flour. Pour over the cooked parsnips, and serve with a sprinkling of pepper.

## Parsnips in Coriander Chive Sauce

*6 parsnips, sliced*
*1 t. coriander*
*½ t. cumin*
*pinch of rosemary (or rue)*
*1 c. parsnip stock*
*¼ c. boiled white wine*
*2 t. olive oil*
*1 T. chopped chives*
*flour*

Cook the parsnips in water, drain, and reserve liquid for stock.

For the sauce, grind together coriander, cumin and rosemary (or rue). Blend with stock, boiled wine, and olive oil. Add chives. Bring to a boil, simmer gently for 10 minutes, and thicken with flour. Serve over the cooked parsnips.

### Parsnips Cooked in Sweet Wine Sauce

*6–8 parsnips*
*water*

Slice parsnips lengthwise and half-cook them in water. Drain and reserve liquid. Finish cooking them in the following sauce.

*Sauce:*
*2 t. olive oil or butter*
*1½ c. parsnip stock*
*½ t. pepper*
*¼ c. sweet raisin wine or muscatel*
*flour*

Combine olive oil or butter, stock, pepper, and sweet wine. Bring to a boil, add parsnips, then simmer together till parsnips are tender. Thicken sauce with flour, and serve with parsnips.

### Carrots Sautéed in Peppered Wine Sauce

*8 medium carrots*
*½ c. white wine*
*½ c. vegetable stock*
*2 t. olive oil*
*½–1 t. pepper*

Thinly slice carrots lengthwise, and sauté them in a mixture of the wine, stock, olive oil, and pepper until done.

Serve carrots with the sauce.

### Carrot Strips Cooked with Cumin

Slice carrots, cook in a little water, then drain. Add olive oil and cumin, to taste, and reheat with the carrots. Serve.

*Do not be misled by the simplicity of this recipe—the results are wonderful. I have found it not essential to precook the carrots since I prefer them crisp. They are excellent served alongside roast chicken with the* Almond Ginger Stuffing for Chicken.

# All Kinds of Dishes

## POTTED SALADS

SALA CATTABIA *Potted Salad* [For the dressing, mix] pepper, mint, celery, dried pennyroyal, cheese, pine nuts, honey, vinegar, stock, egg yolks, and fresh water. In the pot, arrange layers of pressed bread previously soaked in vinegar and water, cheese made from cow's milk, and cucumbers. Strew nuts between the layers. Then add buds of the caper shrub, chopped up very finely, and a layer of little chicken livers. Pour the dressing on top. Chill in ice water and serve.

ALITER SALA CATTABIA APICIANA *Potted Salad Apicius* In a mortar, mix celery seed, dried pennyroyal, dried mint, ginger, green coriander, seedless raisins, honey, vinegar, olive oil, and wine. In the salad bowl, strew pieces of Picentian bread. Arrange the bread in alternate layers with pieces of chicken, goat-kid's glandules, Vestinian cheese, pine nuts, cucumbers, and dried onions chopped very finely. Pour the dressing made above over the potted salad. Strew snow around it until the dinner hour and serve.

ALITER SALA CATTABIA *Potted Salad* Hollow out an Alexandrine loaf and soak the pieces in vinegar and water. Mix in a mortar, pepper, honey, mint, garlic, green coriander, cow's milk cheese seasoned with salt, water, and olive oil. Pack in snow and serve.

## FISH, VEGETABLE, AND FRUIT DISHES

PATINA COTIDIANA *Everyday Dish* Grind cooked brains with pepper, cumin, and laser. Cook with fish-pickle, boiled wine, milk, and eggs over a gentle fire or in warm water. Steam gently.

ALITER PATINA VERSATILIS *Upside-down Dish* Take pine nuts and chopped nuts. Bake these and then grind [and mix] them with honey, pepper, fish-pickle, milk, and eggs. [Cook] in a little olive oil.

ALITER PATINA [*Vegetable Dish*] Pound lettuce stalks. [Mix] with pepper, stock, boiled wine, water, and olive oil. Cook and thicken with eggs. Sprinkle with pepper and serve.

## Tart Potted Salad

(¼ lb. white bread)
(¼ c. mild white wine vinegar)
water
½ c. chopped walnuts or almonds
½ c. grated mozzarella (or other mild) cheese
½ medium cucumber, sliced
¼ c. pickled capers
½ lb. cooked chicken livers, chopped

Soak the bread in vinegar and water, press it, and use it to cover the bottom of a salad bowl. (One may prefer to omit the vinegar soaked bread, and serve this salad with rolls.) Sprinkle with some of the chopped nuts. Cover this with the grated cheese and sprinkle with more nuts. Make a third layer with cucumber slices, a fourth with pickled capers, and a fifth with cooked chicken livers, adding a sprinkling of nuts to each. Chill, and serve with the following dressing.

Dressing:
½ t. chopped fresh mint
dash of ground pepper
pinch of pennyroyal (or mint)
1 t. honey
1 T. almonds, finely chopped
¼ c. white wine vinegar
1 c. olive oil
2 hard-boiled egg yolks
1 c. mild cheese, shredded

Combine chopped mint, pepper, and a pinch of pennyroyal, with honey, chopped nuts, vinegar, and olive oil. Blend with mashed egg yolks. Pour over the salad, and decorate it with shredded cheese. Chill and serve.

*This makes a very rich, delicious main course for a summer garden party.*

## Potted Salad Apicius

*3 c. fine white bread*
*1 c. cooked chicken meat, sliced*
*1 c. cooked sweetbreads, chopped*
*1 c. mild cheese, shredded*
*¼ c. pine nuts or almonds, chopped*
*½ medium cucumber, sliced*
*½ onion, finely chopped*

Cover the bottom of a large salad bowl with some of the white bread. Cover this with sliced chicken. Add a layer of bread. Complete the salad with layers of sweetbreads, shredded cheese, pine nuts or almonds, cucumber slices, and onions chopped very finely, alternating with a layer of bread, as in *Tart Potted Salad.* Chill, and serve with the following dressing.

*Dressing:*
*1 t. celery seed (or ground lovage)*
*pinch of pennyroyal, if available*
*¼ t. mint; pinch of ginger*
*½ t. coriander*
*¼ c. dark raisins*
*1 t. honey*
*2 T. vinegar*
*1 c. olive oil*
*1 T. white wine*

Mix celery seed with pennyroyal, mint, ginger, coriander, raisins, honey, vinegar, olive oil, and white wine. Pour over the salad, and serve.

*If sweetbreads are unavailable this superb cold dish can be made just as well using more chicken meat.*

## Bread Salad

*1 lb. loaf fine white bread*
*3 t. mild vinegar*
*1 c. water*
*1 c. mild cheese, shredded*

Remove the crusts from the loaf of bread, slice, and moisten it with vinegar and water. Cover a shallow salad bowl with pieces of the prepared bread. On top of it, sprinkle a cup of shredded cheese. Chill.

*Dressing:*
*dash of pepper*
*1 t. honey*
*½ t. mint*
*clove of garlic, crushed*
*¼ t. coriander*
*1 c. olive oil*
*2 T. mild white wine vinegar*

To make the dressing combine the pepper, honey, mint, garlic, coriander, olive oil, and vinegar. Pour over the chilled bread, and serve at once.

*An original, "surprise" side dish, with a fresh, lively flavor.*

## "Everyday" Creamed Calf's Brains

1 lb. cooked calf's brains, chopped
½ t. ground pepper
¼ t. cumin
½ t. ginger
dash of fish-pickle (see p. 2)
½ c. boiled white wine
¾ c. milk
2 raw egg yolks

Season brains with pepper, cumin, and ginger. Put into a pan, and combine with fish-pickle, boiled wine, milk, and well beaten egg yolks. Bring to a boil, then simmer together gently until the "everyday" dish has thickened.

*I don't serve this dish every day, but possibly Apicius used the word to mean "ordinary" or "commonplace." I enjoy it served with broccoli, cabbage, or brussel sprouts in a cheese and chive sauce.*

## Nut Omelette

¼ c. roasted chestnuts or almonds, chopped
1 t. honey
pinch of ground pepper
dash of fish-pickle (see p. 2)
½ c. milk
5 raw eggs
2 t. butter or olive oil

Roast chestnuts or almonds for 20 minutes in a 350°F oven. Grind the nuts and mix with honey, pepper, fish-pickle, milk, and eggs. Heat a frying pan, and melt butter or olive oil. Add the omelette mixture. Cook till done.

Alternatively, bind the roasted, ground chestnuts with reduced veal stock and fold into the omelette.

*A simple, satisfying omelette when served for lunch with spinach salad in a vinaigrette dressing.*

## Lettuce Puree

1 head of crisp lettuce, finely chopped
dash of ground pepper
½ c. vegetable stock
¼ c. boiled white wine
2 t. olive oil or butter
2 raw egg yolks

Season fresh lettuce leaves with pepper, and combine with stock, boiled wine, and olive oil or butter. Bring to a boil, then simmer gently for a minute or two. Thicken with the well beaten egg yolks, and serve with a generous sprinkling of pepper.

*An interesting "dip" to serve with raw vegetables, or use as a sauce with cooked fish or chicken.*

## Celery and Brains with Egg Sauce

*1 large bunch of celery, chopped*
*1 lb. cooked calf's brains, chopped*
*1 c. veal stock*
*½ t. ground pepper*
*¼ c. white wine*
*1 raw egg yolk*

Trim, wash, steam, drain, and cool celery (or other fresh greens). Then, in a mixing bowl, season veal stock with pepper. Take the cooked brains, pound them, and combine them with the stock. Now add the celery and wine, and stir together. Pour the celery and brains mixture into a greased cooking pot, heat gently on top of the stove, add well beaten yolk, and simmer till thickened. Serve with a sprinkling of pepper.

## Asparagus Stewed in Wine

*1 lb. asparagus, finely chopped*
*1½ c. white wine*
*¼ t. ground pepper*
*1 t. celery seed (or lovage)*
*1 t. coriander*
*¼ t. savory*
*1 medium onion, chopped*
*2 t. chopped onion*
*1 c. vegetable stock*
*2 t. olive oil*
*1 raw egg yolk*
*ground pepper, to taste*

Take chopped asparagus, pound in a mortar, and steep in wine for about ½ hour. Strain through a colander, reserve wine, and set aside. Now combine pepper, celery seed (or lovage), coriander, savory, onion, ¼ cup of the wine, stock, and olive oil. Pour the asparagus puree and the sauce into a cooking pot, bring to a boil, then simmer gently for 15 minutes. Thicken with well beaten egg yolk. Serve with a sprinkling of finely ground pepper.

## Puree of Watercress or Other Green Vegetables

Puree of watercress (or grape leaves, green mustard plant leaves, cucumber, young cabbage, or cauliflower) is made as in *Asparagus Stewed in Wine*, above. You may wish to put cooked fish or chicken in the dish before adding the prepared vegetable.

## Rose Hips and Calf's Brains Custard

2 c. young rose hips
¼ c. vegetable stock
1 lb. cooked calf's brains,
chopped
½ t. ground pepper
8 small raw eggs
¼ c. red wine
¼ c. sweet raisin wine or
muscatel
½ c. vegetable stock
2 t. olive oil or butter
ground cinnamon

Cook the rose hips for 5 minutes in a little water, drain them, and grind them to a pulp in a mortar. Add stock and strain together through a very fine sieve. (Alternatively, pick seeds out by hand.) Take finely chopped brains and season with pepper. Combine with rose hip juice. In a separate bowl, combine well beaten eggs, wine, sweet wine, stock, and olive oil or butter. Mix brains, seeded rose hips, and the sauce together, and pour all into a greased baking dish. Cook in a 350° F oven for 30 minutes or until firm. Sprinkle with finely ground cinnamon and serve.

## Anchovies Cooked in Herbed Wine

20 fresh (or unsalted,
canned) anchovies
olive oil
½ c. white wine
½ c. fish stock
2 t. olive oil
½ t. rosemary
¼ t. oregano
ground pepper

Wash the anchovies and immerse them in olive oil for 2 hours (or use canned, oil packed, unsalted ones). Then arrange them in a cooking pot with 2 t. of the olive oil. Combine white wine and fish stock with rosemary (or rue) and oregano to taste, add to pot and cook over low heat till fish are done. During cooking spoon the sauce over the fish. Serve with a sprinkling of pepper.

## Steamed Fish Custard

2 lbs. cooked fish fillets
½ t. ground pepper
pinch of rosemary (or
rue)
2 t. olive oil
2 c. fish stock
4 raw eggs

Steam fillets and reserve liquid. Chop them, and put them into a cooking pot. Mix pepper with ground rosemary (or rue), olive oil, and fish stock. Stir this sauce into the fish. Now add well beaten eggs and stir the mixture until it has a smooth texture. Cover and steam over low heat till eggs are firm. Serve with a sprinkling of pepper.

PATINAM EX LACTE  *Milk Casserole*  Steep nuts and dry them. Make sure you have freshly prepared sea urchins on hand. Take a dish, and in it put the ingredients written below into the casserole dish one by one: mallows and beetroots, ripe leeks, celery, freshly boiled greens and vegetable purée, chicken pieces cooked in their own juices, boiled brains, Lucanian sausages, hard-boiled eggs cut in half. Next, add pork sausages made with Terentine sauce, that have been cooked and sliced, chicken livers, fillets of fried codfish, sea nettles, pieces of oyster meat, and fresh cheese. Arrange these ingredients in layers, and then sprinkle each with small nuts and peppercorns. The sauce to be poured over [the dish] is made of these [ingredients]: pepper, lovage, celery seed, and silphium. [Blend these seasonings and] heat. After cooking, strain milk and into it mix raw eggs so that the sauce has a smooth texture. Pour it over the casserole. Cook. When it is cooked, set the fresh sea urchins on top. Sprinkle with pepper and serve.

*Fruitless eggs, which we have termed "wind eggs," are conceived by the imagined passion of the females between themselves or through dust; not only by pigeons, but also by fowls, partridges, peacocks, geese, and Egyptian geese. They are, however, unfruitful, smaller, less pleasing to taste, and more liquid. Some people suspect they are begot by the wind, and for this reason call them "zephyr eggs"; but on the other hand these wind eggs are formed only in the spring when the hens have forsaken brooding. There are also eggs called "cynosura," wind eggs laid in the autumn. Eggs soaked in vinegar are softened to such a degree that they can pass through signet rings. Eggs should be preserved in bean meal or, in winter, in chopped hay and straw. In summer, bran is most beneficial. It is thought that eggs become utterly empty if they are preserved in salt.*

Pliny.

## Milk Casserole

¼ c. almonds or pine nuts
1 t. coarsely ground pepper
6–10 green cabbage or grape
leaves (or mallow leaves),
parboiled
3–4 beets, sliced
1 c. leeks, sliced
½ c. celery, chopped
½ c. cooked peas or beans
½ lb. cooked chicken
½ c. cooked calf's brains,
chopped
Lucanian Spiced Sausage (see
p. 15)
3 hard-boiled eggs
½ c. pork sausage slices
½ c. Terentine Sauce (see
p. 132)
½ c. cooked chicken livers,
chopped
½ c. poached cod fillets
5 ozs. small raw oysters,
chopped
½ c. cottage cheese
5 sea urchins (the freshly
cooked meats), see p. 174

Sauce:
pinch of ground pepper
¼ t. lovage (or celery seed)
½ t. celery seed
fennel
2 raw eggs
1 c. milk

Steep nuts in water for an hour, drain them, and season each layer of the casserole with some of them combined with ground pepper.

In a casserole, carefully arrange the following ingredients in layers: a few parboiled grape, cabbage (or mallow) leaves, beets, leeks, celery, and peas, or beans, or other cooked green vegetable. On these prepared vegetables, place slices of boned chicken cooked in their own juices, cooked calf's brains, and a few slices of Lucanian sausage. Add hard-boiled egg halves, a layer of sliced pork sausage mixed with the following Terentine sauce, cooked chicken livers, poached cod fillets, and oysters. Finish with the cottage cheese.

*This casserole is a superb tour de force. The enormous number of flavors makes a single serving an aesthetic and culinary experience. I suggest serving it at the meeting of an historical society or to dinner guests who will truly appreciate its complexity. Simply assembling the ingredients takes half a day!*

To make the sauce, grind pepper with lovage (or celery seed) and celery seed in a mortar. Add fennel to taste. In a pan, combine with well beaten eggs and milk. Stir and heat. Pour this sauce over the casserole. Decorate with the sea urchins. Cook, covered, for 40 minutes to 1 hour in a 350°F oven until vegetables are done.

45

## Casserole Apicius with Meat or Fish

*Pancakes:*
*3 eggs*
*½ c. flour*
*⅓ c. milk*
*⅓ c. water*

To make 6 pancakes beat 3 eggs, and add the flour, milk, and water to make a thin batter. Into a greased 8 inch frying pan, pour a little of the batter and allow it to spread evenly. Cook each pancake over high heat and flip over when it is lightly browned.

*1½ lbs. cooked fish fillets (sole,*
*halibut, turbot, or salmon)*
*or 2½ c. cooked pork, or*
*chicken, thinly sliced*
*3 raw eggs*
*2 T. olive oil*
*½ t. ground pepper*
*½ t. celery seed (or lovage)*
*2 c. beef or chicken stock*
*¼ c. white wine*
*¼ c. sweet raisin wine or*
*muscatel*
*flour*
*coarsely ground pepper*
*pine nuts or almonds*

Prepare cooked meat or fish. Mix these with the eggs, olive oil, celery seed (or lovage), stock, white wine, and sweet wine. Heat the meats in this sauce, adding more liquid if required. Thicken sauce with flour.

Next, take a greased casserole dish and cover the bottom with a layer of meats or fish in their sauce. Sprinkle with coarsely ground pepper and with nuts. On this, place a pancake. Fill the dish with layers of the sauced meats, seasoned with pepper and nuts, each alternating with a pancake. Pierce a hole in the final pancake to allow steam to escape and cook uncovered in a 375° F oven for 20–25 minutes until the dish is uniformly heated. Serve with a sprinkling of pepper.

*An astonishingly rich dish, with interesting textures and gentle flavors.*

## Fish with Meats in Seasoned Cheese Sauce

*1 lb. fish fillets*
*olive oil*
*1 c. cooked calf's brains, chopped*
*1 c. chicken livers*
*4 hard-boiled eggs, chopped*
*1 c. melted mild white cheese*

Lightly sauté fish fillets in olive oil, debone, and break the fillets into pieces. Heat these together with chopped calf's brains, chicken livers, hard-boiled eggs, and melted cheese. (The cheese may first be steeped in vinegar and thyme.)

*Sauce:*
*dash of ground pepper*
*¼ t. celery seed (or lovage)*
*½ t. oregano*
*2 rue berries (or peppercorns)*
*1 t. honey (or mead)*
*¼ c. wine*
*2 t. olive oil*
*1 c. stock*
*2 raw egg yolks*
*butter*
*ground cumin*

Meanwhile, grind together, in a mortar, pepper, celery seed (or lovage), oregano, and a couple of rue berries (or peppercorns). Combine with honey (or mead), wine, and olive oil. Thicken this sauce with well beaten yolks and add to the first dish. Cook in a buttered casserole for 20 to 30 minutes in a 375°F oven. Serve with a sprinkling of cumin (or sprinkle on top while cooking).

### Steamed Green Vegetables with Pepper & Thyme

*1 large bunch of celery,*
*1 medium cabbage,*
*2 large heads of broccoli*

Take celery, cabbage, or other green vegetable, and steam in a little water till cooked. Spread the vegetable in a shallow pan.

*Sauce:*
*dash of ground pepper*
*1–1½ t. celery seed (or lovage)*
*¼ t. coriander*
*pinch of savory*
*2 t. chopped onion*
*½ c. white wine*
*1 c. vegetable stock*
*1 t. white wine vinegar or cider vinegar*
*2 t. olive oil*
*flour*
*ground thyme*
*ground pepper*

For the sauce, grind the pepper, celery seed (or lovage), coriander, and savory together in a mortar. Add to the onion, wine, stock, vinegar, and olive oil. Pour this sauce over the green vegetable. Heat and simmer gently for 5 minutes, then thicken sauce with flour. Sprinkle the dish with thyme and pepper, and serve.

*Though Apicius added a dash of baking soda to restore the color of the greens, it is omitted here as some vitamins are destroyed in the process. This savory sauce enormously enhances our most common green vegetables.*

### Wine-Fried Anchovies

*6 oz. fresh anchovies (or unsalted, canned anchovies)*
*1 raw egg, lightly beaten*
*1 T. olive oil*
*¼ c. white wine*
*¼ c. fish stock*

Wash and trim the anchovies and brush them with egg. In the frying pan, heat olive oil with wine and stock added. When the pan is very hot, add the anchovies and cook them lightly. Serve with a sprinkling of pepper.

### Brains and Salted Fish

½ lb. salted (or fresh) cod,
tuna, or sturgeon
4 hard-boiled eggs
1 c. cooked calf's brains
1 c. cooked chicken livers

(Soak the salted fish in water before using it in this dish.) Chop the hard-boiled eggs, brains, and chicken livers. Set this mixture in a stew pot, with the fish in the middle.

Sauce:
¼ t. ground pepper
¼ t. celery seed (or lovage)
½ c. sweet raisin wine
or muscatel
½ c. veal or chicken stock
pinch of rosemary (or rue),
or sage
flour

To make the sauce, mix the pepper, celery seed (or lovage), sweet wine, and stock. Add rosemary, rue, or sage. Bring to a boil and pour over the prepared meats. Simmer together over low heat until fish is tender. Thicken the sauce with flour, and serve.

*This sauce will also be very good used with any single one of the main ingredients.*

### Red Mullet Sautéed in Wine

1 lb. red mullet fillets
2 T. olive oil or butter
½ c. sweet raisin wine or
mead

Sauté the mullet fillets in olive oil or butter. While they are cooking, season each fillet with a tablespoon of mead or sweet wine. Serve with a sprinkling of pepper.

### Fish Poached with Shallots

1 lb. fish fillets
6 shallots
1 c. fish stock
2 T. olive oil or butter
white wine vinegar or cider
vinegar
parsley

Put the fish on a bed of shallots in a pan. Add fish stock and olive oil or butter, sufficient to reach half way up the fish. Poach the fillets till done. Place the cooked fish in the middle of a platter, sprinkle with vinegar, decorate with parsley, and serve.

*This makes an exciting light lunch for two. Accompany with a chilled Chablis or Bordeaux, with cheese and coffee to follow.*

## Fish with Sweet and Sour Onions Lucretius

*6 shallots or sweet onions*
*1 c. fish stock*
*2 T. olive oil*
*water*
*1 lb. fish fillets (sole, cod, salmon)*
*1 t. honey*
*1 t. white wine vinegar or cider vinegar*
*1 t. boiled wine*
*fish-pickle (see p. 2)*
*honey*
*parsley*

Take shallots or sweet onions, discard the tops, and chop into a cooking pot. Moisten this bed of onions with stock, olive oil, and a little water. Place pieces of uncooked fish in the middle, bring to a boil, then cook gently over low heat, basting the fish from time to time. When nearly done, season with honey, vinegar, and boiled wine. (Taste and correct for blandness with fish-pickle and for saltiness with honey). Decorate the dish with parsley and serve.

*A delicious marrying of sweet and sour flavors.*

## Fish Fillets with Leeks and Coriander

*2 lbs. raw fish fillets or steaks*
*1 c. fish stock*
*1 c. boiled white wine*
*1 T. olive oil*
*1 c. sliced leeks*
*1 t. coriander*
*½ t. ground pepper*
*½ t. celery seed (or lovage)*
*½ t. oregano*
*2 raw egg yolks*

Take fish fillets, chop into pieces, and put into a pot. Add stock, boiled wine, olive oil, and leeks. Bring to a boil, then simmer over low heat. Meanwhile, grind together coriander, pepper, celery seed (or lovage), and oregano. Add these seasonings to the stew. Thicken the liquid by adding well beaten yolks little by little. Simmer for 10 minutes. Serve with a sprinkling of pepper.

*An easy but very elegant way to serve fish.*

PATELLAM LUCRETIANAM *A Lucretian Dish* Wash onions. Throw out the green parts and slice [the onions which remain] into a cooking vessel. Add a little fish stock, olive oil, and water. While [the onions are] cooking, place raw saltfish in their midst. And when the [stewed onions and] fish are almost cooked, sprinkle a spoonful of honey and just a touch of vinegar and boiled wine. Taste. If the dish is bland, add a little fish-pickle. If it should be too salty, add a little honey [to temper it]. Sprinkle with the leaves of the oxtongue plant and simmer.

℧ This dish is named after Titus Lucretius Carus (99–55 B.C.), the greatest philosopher/poet to write in Latin. He believed in the philosophical system of the Greek Epicurus, who tried to replace religion with a doctrine of natural causes. Ethically, this led to the conclusion that pleasure was the only good, to be attained by the harmony between mind and body which resulted from moderation and virtue. But those devoted to sensual pleasures saw in Lucretius a justification for their behavior and this is the modern sense of the word "epicure." It is ironic that Apicius should name a dish after Lucretius, who would have heartily despised him.

## Fillet of Sole with Wine and Oregano

*1 lb. fresh fillets of sole*
*2 T. olive oil or butter*
*¼ c. fish stock*
*¼ c. white wine*

Take fillets and arrange them in a pan with the olive oil or butter, fish stock, and white wine. Cook lightly.

*Sauce:*
*dash of ground pepper*
*½ t. celery seed (or lovage)*
*¼ t. oregano*
*1 c. fish stock*
*2 raw egg yolks*

Meanwhile, for the sauce, grind together pepper, celery seed (or lovage), and oregano. Add to stock and well beaten yolks. Stir and pour over the fish. Finish the fillets in the sauce over low heat, and serve with a sprinkling of pepper.

*The sauce is delicate, and you may wish to add more oregano if the herb is a favorite. Serve with small boiled potatoes and buttered peas.*

## Fish Cooked with Raisins and Wine

*½ lb. cooked fresh tuna, fresh sardines, or anchovies*

For the sauce grind together in a mortar, pepper, celery seed (or lovage), and oregano. Add to onion, white wine, fish stock and olive oil. Pour the sauce into a pot, bring to a boil and simmer 20 minutes over low heat. Then add the cooked fish. Cook together for a few minutes more, then thicken sauce with flour and serve together.

*Sauce:*
*¼ c. dark raisins*
*dash of ground pepper*
*½ t. celery seed (or lovage)*
*½ t. oregano*
*2 t. chopped onion*
*½ c. white wine*
*1 c. fish stock*
*2 T. olive oil*
*flour*

*Though tuna is ubiquitous in our kitchens it need not be sentenced to the ignominy of a sandwich or a bit part in a casserole. Apicius here balanced green herbs with the tang of pepper and onion, and the smoothness of white wine, then added the surprise of raisins. This sauce transforms the taste of the tuna without dominating it.*

## Fish with Oysters in Wine Sauce

*1 lb. poached fish fillets*
*(bream, mullet, golden*
*shiner)*
*½ c. oyster meats, chopped*
*¼ t. ground pepper*
*1 c. fish stock*
*½ c. white wine*
*3 T. olive oil or butter*
*1 raw egg yolk*

Lightly poach fish fillets, cut in pieces and set aside. Shuck and chop enough raw oysters to yield ½ cup of meat. In a mortar, grind pepper and add to fish stock and white wine. Put this wine sauce into a pan with olive oil, bring to a boil, and simmer for 10 minutes to reduce. Add the oysters, and cook for 2–3 minutes in the sauce. Now put the fish and oysters into a cooking pot along with reduced sauce from the pan. Cook together gently over low heat for a few minutes more, thickening with well beaten yolk. Serve with a sprinkling of pepper.

## Pike Fillets in Cumin Wine Sauce

*1 lb. poached pike fillets*
*fish stock*

*Sauce:*
*dash of ground pepper*
*½ t. cumin*
*1 T. chopped parsley*
*pinch of rosemary (or rue)*
*2 t. chopped onion*
*1 t. honey*
*1 c. fish stock*
*¼ c. sweet white wine*
*1 t. olive oil*

To make the sauce, in a mortar, grind pepper with cumin and rosemary (or rue). Add to parsley and onion. Blend with honey, stock, sweet wine, and olive oil. Bring to a boil, then simmer gently for 25 minutes to reduce.

Meanwhile, take pike fillets and poach them in fish stock. To serve, arrange fillets on a platter and pour the sauce over them.

## *Apples and Calf's Brains Casserole*

2 lbs. apples (or serviceberries)
½ lb. cooked calf's brains, chopped
dash of ground pepper
½ c. beef or chicken stock
2 raw eggs
ginger or cinnamon
butter

Take serviceberries or apples, wash, peel and pound the fruit in a mortar, and strain through a colander (or put through a blender). Then season the brains with pepper. Add the mashed fruit and combine, binding the mixture together with well beaten eggs and sufficient stock. Grease a casserole dish, place the fruit and meat mixture in it, and cook for 30 minutes in a 375° F oven. Serve with a sprinkling of ginger or cinnamon. Alternatively, chill and serve cold.

*Calf's brains today are not for everyone, yet they are unassuming, and really just a vehicle for herbs and spices. This dish makes a splendid change of pace between the fish and meat courses at a formal dinner.*

## *Peaches Cooked with Cumin*

Take early peaches, wash, cut them in quarters, and remove pits. Steam in water until soft. Drain, reserve liquid, and put them in a cooking pot with a little of the peach liquid, a few drops of olive oil, and cumin to taste. Simmer gently for a few minutes and serve hot.

*Apicius cooked peaches with cumin, and preserved them with savory. For an exciting summertime dessert season a dish of raw peach slices with liquid honey, cumin, mint, and savory. Chill, and top with whipped cream. The children in my cooking classes love this dish.*

## Pears Cooked with Cinnamon and Wine

*1 lb. pears*
*water*
*1 t. cinnamon*
*pinch of cumin*
*2 T. honey*
*½ c. sweet white wine*
*1 T. olive oil or butter*
*1 c. pear liquid*
*2 egg yolks*
*nutmeg*

Take pears, wash, peel, and steam in water till soft. Drain and reserve liquid. Remove the pear cores, and quarter them. Put the pieces into a pot, and season with cinnamon, cumin, honey, sweet white wine, olive oil or butter, and the pear liquid from the steaming pan. Simmer gently for a few minutes. Thicken liquid with well beaten yolks. Serve hot with a sprinkling of nutmeg.

*Apicius was masterful in his use of spices with fruit. In this recipe the piquant taste of a little cumin accents the fruit, and acts as a counterpoint to the cinnamon and nutmeg.*

## Hot or Cold Spinach (or Nettle) Quiche

*1 c. spinach or nettles*
*butter*
*½ c. fresh mushrooms, sliced*
*1 c. cheddar cheese, grated*
*1 medium onion, sliced in*
*rings*
*½ c. flour*
*1 T. fish-pickle (see p. 2)*
*3 raw eggs*
*1 ½ c. cream*
*1 t. coriander*
*½ t. pepper, coarsely ground*

Take a bunch of fresh spinach, or pick a basket of young spring nettles, and steam until tender. Drain and chop 1 cup of the spinach or nettles. Arrange in a buttered quiche pan. Cover with layers of mushrooms, cheese, and onion. Now blend the flour, fish-pickle, well beaten eggs, cream, coriander, and pepper. Pour the mixture over the dry ingredients in the quiche pan. Bake in a 400°F oven for 35 to 40 minutes, and serve hot with a sprinkling of pepper. Alternatively, chill and serve cold.

*By early April the damp shady alder bottom acres on my farm are covered in a green sea of young nettles. This is when they are at their best, before the sun coarsens them.*

## Quinces Stewed with Leeks

*1 lb. quinces*
*water*
*½ c. leeks, sliced*
*2 T. honey*
*1 T. olive oil or butter*
*¼ c. boiled white wine*
*quince liquid*

Take ripe quinces, quarter, peel them, put in a pot, cover with water, and cook for 45 minutes. Reserve the liquid, then put the quinces in another pot. Add sliced leeks, honey, olive oil or butter, boiled wine, and sufficient liquid from the first pan to cover the fruit. Cook gently, covered, over low heat for ½ hour or until done.

Alternatively, the quinces can be stewed simply in honey diluted with liquid from the boiling pan.

*Leeks are a splendid vegetable, versatile and fond of company. Very good served with roast pork or ham.*

## Spiced Seafood Dumplings

*1 lb. fish fillets*
*2 T. olive oil*
*¼ c. white wine*
*1 c. reduced fish stock*
*2 heads of leeks, finely chopped*
*1 t. coriander*
*½ c. flour*
*¼ c. fish stock*
*dash of ground pepper*
*½ t. celery seed (or lovage)*
*½ t. oregano*
*(flour)*

Place fish fillets in a pot and poach lightly in a mixture of olive oil, white wine, and reduced fish stock. Remove the fish, reserve liquid, and flake it. Mix with chopped leeks, coriander, flour, and fish stock, if needed. Shape into small balls of forcemeat. Put the fish dumplings into a buttered casserole, cover, and cook gently in a 325°F oven for 20 minutes.

Meanwhile, in a mortar, grind pepper, celery seed (or lovage), and oregano. Combine with liquid from the pan of cooked fish. Pour over the dumplings. Cook for a further 10 minutes, and then, if you wish thicken the liquid with flour. Serve with a sprinkling of pepper.

## Meatball Ragout Terentine

*1 lb. very small cooked beef or pork meatballs*
*4 heads of leeks, sliced*
*2 t. olive oil*
*½ c. reduced beef stock*
*1 c. vegetable stock*

First cook small beef or pork meatballs in a pan in olive oil.

Into a casserole put leeks. Add olive oil, reduced stock, vegetable stock, and cooked meat balls. Cook with the following sauce.

*Sauce:*
*¼ c. red wine*
*¼ c. sweet raisin wine or muscatel*
*pinch of ground pepper*
*1 t. celery seed (or lovage)*
*½ t. oregano*
*2 T. pastry flour*
*¼ c. water*

To make the sauce, combine the red wine, sweet or raisin wine, pepper, celery seed (or lovage), and oregano. Pour over the ragout. Cover and cook in a 325°F oven for 30 to 40 minutes. Combine flour and water and add to the dish to thicken it. Serve with a sprinkling of pepper.

*A delicious wine flavored sauce, with the spicy addition of lovage or celery seed.*

## Ragout Apicius with Fishes and Meats

*½ lb. fresh small fish (fresh anchovies, sardines, etc.)*
*1 c. (uncooked) ground pork dumplings*
*½ c. cooked chicken livers, diced*
*1 pair sweetbreads, chopped*
*2 T. olive oil*
*1 c. meat stock*
*½ c. white wine*
*4 heads of leeks, chopped*
*1 t. of mint*

*Sauce:*
*¼ t. ground pepper*
*½ t. celery seed (or lovage)*
*½ t. coriander*
*1 T. honey*
*½ c. white wine*
*flour*

In a casserole, put olive oil, stock, wine, leeks, mint, whole cleaned fish, pork dumplings, chicken livers, and sweetbreads. Cover and cook in a 350°F oven for an hour, adding stock if necessary.

Meanwhile, for the sauce, grind pepper, celery seed (or lovage), and coriander. Moisten with some gravy from the ragout. Blend with honey and white wine. Heat this sauce and pour it over the ragout. Continue cooking for a few minutes, then finish by thickening the liquid with flour. Sprinkle with pepper and serve.

*An exciting combination of fish and meats, whose flavors are tied together with the spiced sauce. Some may prefer not to thicken the sauce as Apicius did.*

## Matius' Ragout with Ham and Apples

½ lb. small (uncooked) ground pork dumplings
1 lb. cooked ham, diced
2 t. olive oil
1 c. beef or pork stock
½ c. reduced beef or pork stock
2 leeks, sliced
½ t. coriander
2 c. apples, diced

In a deep casserole, put olive oil, stock, and reduced stock. To these ingredients add leeks, coriander, and pork meatballs. Dice the cooked ham and add to the ragout. Cook, covered, in a 350°F oven for 1 hour. After 45 minutes, add peeled, diced apples, and cook 15 minutes more.

Then make the following sauce and finish together.

Sauce:
pinch of ground pepper
¼ t. cumin
½ t. coriander
1 t. of mint
¼ t. ginger
1 t. wine vinegar or cider vinegar
1 t. honey or sugar
½ c. beef or pork stock
¼ c. boiled wine
¼ c. casserole juices
flour

For the sauce, in a mortar grind pepper, cumin, coriander, mint, and ginger. Moisten these seasonings with vinegar. Combine with honey, stock, boiled wine, and liquid from the casserole. Bring this sauce to a boil, then pour it over the apples and pork. Continue cooking for a few minutes, then thicken with flour. Serve with a sprinkling of pepper.

*I like to complement* Matius' Ragout with Ham and Apples *with a glass of medium sweet cider, but you may prefer a glass of white wine. Be careful to use only ham which has been cured without excessive salt.*

## Sweet Citron Ragout of Ham and Pork

*1 lb. cooked ham, diced*
*½ lb. (uncooked) ground*
*pork*
*2 t. olive oil*
*1 c. beef or pork stock*
*½ c. reduced beef or*
*pork stock*
*2 heads of leeks, chopped*
*½ t. coriander*

In a casserole, put olive oil, stock, reduced stock, leeks, coriander, cooked ham, and pork meatballs. Cook, covered, in a 350°F oven for 1 hour.

*Sauce:*
*pinch of ground pepper*
*¼ t. cumin*
*½ t. coriander*
*pinch of rosemary (or rue)*
*¼ t. ginger*
*1 t. wine vinegar*
*¼ c. boiled wine*
*¼ c. casserole juices*
*½ c. beef or pork stock*
*½ T. diced lemon (or*
*citron) peel*
*honey*
*flour*

For the sauce, in a mortar, grind pepper with cumin, coriander, rosemary (or rue), and ginger. Moisten with the vinegar. In a pan, add to boiled wine, liquid from the casserole, and stock. Bring the sauce to a boil, take diced lemon (or citron), add to sauce, and simmer for 20 minutes. Pour into the ragout and cook together 15 minutes more. (If lemon peel is used, add honey to taste.) To finish the dish thicken sauce with flour. Serve with a sprinkling of pepper.

*Delicious for lunch with a lettuce and spinach salad, and a bottle of Sauterne. The citron in Roman times was sweet enough to be eaten with a sprinkle of vinegar. I like to lend this recipe a touch of vivacity through the use of lemon peel.*

### Ham and Apricot Ragout

*1 lb. cooked ham, diced*
*2 t. olive oil*
*1 c. pork stock*
*¼ c. white wine*
*¼ c. shallots, chopped*

In a casserole, put ham, olive oil, stock, wine, and shallots. Cook, covered, in the oven for 1 hour.

*Sauce:*
*pinch each of pepper and cumin*
*1 sprig of mint*
*pinch of aniseed*
*1 T. honey*
*¼ c. pork stock*
*¼ c. sweet raisin wine or muscatel*
*1 t. wine vinegar*
*¼ c. casserole liquid*
*10 fresh apricots (or dried, pre-soaked in water)*
*flour*
*ground pepper*

To make the sauce, in a mortar, grind pepper with cumin, mint, and aniseed. Combine with honey, stock, sweet wine, vinegar, and liquid from the casserole. Bring the sauce to a boil and add to the ragout for the last 15 minutes.

When ragout is nearly done, take the apricots, divide in half, and pit them. Add them to the casserole and cook together for 5 minutes. Finish by thickening with flour. Serve with a sprinkling of pepper.

*Apicius'* Ham and Apricot Ragout *is unusual, full of exciting flavors, and typical of a cuisine which freely mixes meats and fruits on the stove.*

*For a chilled dessert after this ragout take prepared apricots and add peach, pear, or apricot juice, torn mint leaves, a little cumin, liquid honey and Muscatel wine. Put in the fridge for an hour, then serve with whipped cream on top.*

## Barley Soup with Meat

*½ c. pearl barley or wheat berries*
*10 c. water*
*2 T. olive oil*
*1 t. aniseed (tied in cheesecloth)*
*½ t. savory*
*1 pig's knuckle (or 3 lbs. lamb or mutton bones)*
*½ t. coriander*
*¼ t. ground pepper*
*½ t. celery seed (or lovage)*
*pinch each of mint (or pennyroyal) and fennel*
*½ t. cumin*
*1 t. wine vinegar*
*½ c. boiled white wine*

Soak barley or wheat for 24 hours in water, then rinse. Put it in a pan and cook till tender together with water, olive oil, the small bouquet garni of aniseed, savory, and the knuckle or bones to flavor the broth. Add coriander, and salt to taste. Remove the bouquet garni of aniseed. In a mortar, grind pepper, celery seed (or lovage), mint (or pennyroyal), cumin, and fennel. Moisten with vinegar and combine with boiled white wine. Pour into the barley soup and simmer over very low heat for at least 2 hours more.

## Vegetable and Lentil Soup

*1 c. chick-peas*
*1 c. lentils*
*1 c. green peas*
*½ c. barley (pre-soaked)*
*10 c. water*
*2 T. olive oil*
*2 heads of leeks, finely chopped*
*½ t. coriander*
*pinch each of aniseed and fennel*
*½ c. beets, diced*
*4 grape (or mallow) leaves, chopped*
*½ c. cabbage leaves, chopped*
*½ t. oregano*
*pinch of fennel*
*pinch of celery seed (or lovage)*
*½ t. honey*
*¼ c. cabbage leaves, chopped*

Soak barley for 24 hours in water, then rinse. Into a pot, put chick-peas, lentils, and peas. Add drained barley to the legumes, together with water and olive oil. To this, add heads of leeks, coriander, aniseed, fennel, beets, grape (or mallow) leaves, and cabbage leaves. Cook gently over low heat for at least 3 hours. One half hour before the soup is cooked, grind together oregano, fennel, and celery seed (or lovage), and add to the soup. Stir. Simmer ½ hour and serve with a garnish of chopped raw cabbage leaves.

*These soups, originally designed for invalids, are delicious, and always seem to taste better reheated on the second day. For someone with a cold I increase the quantities of celery seed or lovage, and oregano.*

## Upside-down Mixed Hors D'oeuvres

*8 cabbage, grape (or mallow) leaves, parboiled*
*4 beets, diced*
*2 leeks, finely chopped*
*3 stalks celery, chopped*
*6 whole small onions*
*7 poached snails*
*½ c. chicken livers, chopped*
*½ c. cooked chicken breast (or bird meats), thinly sliced*
*10 damsons or plums*
*1 c. Chicken Forcemeats (see p. 12)*
*½ c. Lucanian sausage (see p. 15), thinly sliced*
*olive oil or butter*
*¼ c. white wine*
*1 c. chicken stock*
*dash of wine vinegar*

*First sauce:*
*dash of ground pepper*
*½ t. celery seed (or lovage)*
*pinch of ginger & chamomile*
*½ c. white wine*
*3 raw egg yolks*

*Second sauce:*
*dash of ground pepper*
*¼ t. celery seed (or lovage)*
*½ c. chicken stock*
*½ c. white wine*
*¼ c. sweet raisin wine or muscatel*
*olive oil*

Take a deep casserole, and grease it with olive oil. Spread grape (or mallow) leaves on the bottom and along the sides. Arrange the green vegetables and the beets as a first layer. Allow a little room between the vegetables. Now bruise the onions in a mortar and add them to the green vegetables. Carefully place on this the prepared snails, halved and pitted damsons, the chicken dumplings, and thinly sliced sausage. Moisten with olive oil or butter, wine, and stock. Add vinegar to taste.

To the casserole, add the following sauce, but reserve a little. Combine pepper, celery seed (or lovage), ginger, chamomile (or pellitory), and wine. Add well beaten egg yolks to the remaining sauce, and pour this atop the antepast. Cook the covered casserole in a 350°F oven for 1 hour or until done.

Now make the second sauce by combining pepper, celery seed (or lovage), stock, wine, and sweet wine. Bring the wine sauce to a boil, adding a little olive oil. Thicken with flour. Turn the cooked dish upside down onto a serving dish, remove the leaves, and pour some of the wine sauce over it. Serve with a sprinkling of pepper, and the rest of the sauce.

*The list of ingredients required to make this feast dish is immense, and its preparation constitutes a sort of culinary marathon. You need no more than a single portion with, perhaps, a little bread, to be satisfied. It is like an archeological dig, since one slice reveals a profile of the incredible variety of Apicius' cuisine.*

## Liver, Chicken, and Onion Hors D'oeuvres

*3 medium onions*
*1 c. chicken stock*
*2 T. olive oil*
*½ c. white wine*
*1 c. pork and chicken livers, sliced*
*3 cooked chicken breasts, sliced*

In a deep pot, poach onions in stock, olive oil, and white wine till done. Combine with sliced livers and chicken. Put all in a casserole and cook for 1 hour in a 375°F oven.

*Sauce:*
*dash of pepper*
*½ t. celery seed (or lovage)*
*1 c. chicken stock*
*¼ c. white wine*
*flour*

When the meats are almost cooked, combine pepper, celery seed (or lovage), stock, and white wine for the sauce. Add a little liquid from the casserole dish and bring the sauce to a boil. Take the onions out and pour the sauce over the meats. Bring to a boil, thicken with flour if you wish, and serve.

## Sweet Apricot Hors D'oeuvres

*1 lb. hard-ripe apricots*

Take washed apricots, halve and pit them, and put them in a stew pot.

*Sauce:*
*1 t. mint*
*1 t. cinnamon*
*3 t. honey*
*½ c. sweet raisin wine or muscatel*
*½ c. white wine*
*1 t. white wine vinegar*
*1 T. olive oil*
*flour*
*cinnamon or nutmeg*

For the sauce, first mix mint and cinnamon. Blend with honey, sweet wine, and vinegar. Pour the sauce over the apricots, add olive oil, cover, and stew over very low heat for ½ hour or until done. When cooked, thicken liquid with flour. Sprinkle cinnamon or nutmeg over the apricot hors d'oeuvres, and serve.

*Alternatively, for a dessert, halve ripe apricots into a dish with apricot, peach or pear juice. Season with mint, cinnamon, and liquid honey. Chill, and top with whipped cream. The perfect finish to a Roman meal.*

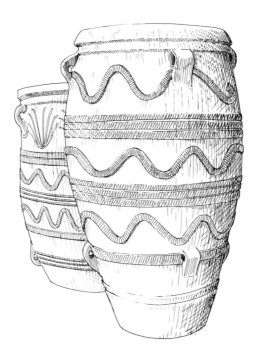

# Legumes

## Book Five

### POTTAGES

¶ Pottages were made of a variety of pulse, or legumes, and grains and were considered by Pliny to be the foods eaten by the earliest Romans. Pottages antedated the discovery of bread-making in Rome, giving rise to the term "pultiphagus" (pottage eater) meaning "a Roman."

*It is evident that Romans lived for a long time not on bread but on pottage, since even now foods are called "pulmentaria" [pottages]. And Ennius, the most ancient Roman poet, recounts as he is describing a famine in Rome caused by a siege, how fathers snatched morsels of pottage out of the hands of their crying children. Consequently the oldest sacred rites and birthdays are celebrated with sacrificial pottage.*

Pliny.

PULTES IULIANAE SIC COQUUNTUR *Pottage Julian* Pour purified spelt into a saucepan. [Add water and] bring to the boil. While boiling, add olive oil. When [the mixture] thickens, stir until the surface is smooth. Now mix two cooked brains with a half pound of meat, ground as for forcemeats. Put this into a pan. [In a mortar] mix pepper, lovage, fennel seed, stock, and a little wine. Add this sauce to the brains and forcemeat, and cook. Afterwards, stir the mixture into the pottage. From this preparation the spelt is made savory. Add it by the ladleful and stir carefully until the pottage has the appearance of a paste.

PULTES CUM IURE OENOCOCTI *Pottage in Wine Sauce* Season the pottage with wine sauce, season cooked fine wheat flour or spelt in this sauce, and serve with tender pieces of pork made savory by the wine sauce.

PULTES TRACTOGALATAE *Pottage of Pastry and Milk* Put a pint of milk and a little water in a clean saucepan and heat over a slow fire. Take three circles of dry bread, crumble them, and add them to the milk. To avoid scorching, mix and stir with water. When it has cooked fully on the stove, add honey. A similar pottage can be made with must and milk, salt, and a little olive oil.

PULTES *Pottage* Pour [a quantity of] purified spelt into a saucepan. [Add water and] bring to a boil. When hot, add olive oil. When the mixture thickens, blend [in a mixing bowl] two cooked brains and a half pound of meat ground as for forcemeats. Mix with the brains and put them in a saucepan. [In a mortar] grind pepper, lovage, and fennel seed. Add stock and a little unmixed wine, and pour over the brains and meats. Afterwards, stir the mixture into the pottage. Little by little, make the spelt savory with this preparation. Stir carefully until [the pottage] has the appearance of a paste.

## LENTILS

*I find the authorities on the subject consider that the eating of lentils promotes an even temper.*

Pliny.

LENTICULA EX SPHONDYLIS *Lentils and Parsnips* [Boil the lentils and put them in] a fresh pan. In a mortar, put pepper, cumin, coriander seed, mint, rue, and pennyroyal. Grind. Pour vinegar over [these seasonings]. Add honey, stock, and boiled wine. Mix with vinegar. Pour this sauce into the pan. Add mashed, boiled parsnips, and cook. When well cooked, thicken [with starch] and serve in a mushroom dish with fresh olive oil.

LENTICULAM DE CASTANEIS *Lentils with Chestnuts* [Boil the lentils.] Take a clean saucepan and put carefully washed chestnuts into it. Add water and a little soda, and cook. When cooked, put pepper, cumin, coriander seed, mint, rue, laser root, and pennyroyal into a mortar. Bruise [these seasonings together]. Pour vinegar over them, and also honey and stock. Blend with [more] vinegar. Pour the sauce over the cooked chestnuts. [Add the lentils.] Add olive oil. Bring to the boil. Stir and taste. If anything is lacking, add it now. When you have poured [the lentils and chestnuts] into a mushroom dish, add fresh olive oil.

## Calf's Brains with Fennel Pottage

*2 T. wholewheat pastry flour*
*1 c. water*
*2 T. olive oil or butter*
*¼ lb. cooked calf's brains, chopped*
*½ lb. ground beef*
*½ t. ground pepper*
*½ t. celery seed (or lovage)*
*pinch of fennel seed*
*1 c. beef stock*
*¼ c. white wine*

For the pottage, put flour into a pan with water. Bring to a boil, stirring frequently. Add olive oil or butter, stir till smooth, and keep warm. Now mix chopped calf's brains with ground meat and shape into dumplings. Put the meats into a fresh pan and cook in a mixture of pepper, celery seed (or lovage), fennel seed, stock, and wine. When the meats are cooked and seasoned in this sauce, add them spoonful by spoonful to the pottage, and serve.

*This dish had ancient sources even in Apicius' time, since the thick pottage or gruel was believed to be the precurser of bread, and eaten by the earliest Romans.*

## Lentils and Chestnuts in Coriander Wine Sauce

*1 c. lentils*
*2½ c. beef or vegetable stock*
*1 c. shelled chestnuts*
*½ t. ground pepper*
*¼ t. cumin*
*½ t. coriander*
*1 t. mint*
*pinch of rosemary (or rue), fennel, and pennyroyal, if available*
*1 t. wine vinegar*
*1 T. honey*
*1 c. vegetable or beef stock*
*2 T. olive oil or butter*

Cook lentils in stock till tender. Drain, reserve stock, and set lentils aside. Take a fresh pan and put chestnuts into it. Cover with water, simmer till cooked, drain, and slice.

Meanwhile, in a mortar, grind pepper, cumin, coriander, mint, and a pinch of rosemary (or rue), fennel, and pennyroyal. Moisten with vinegar and blend with honey. Put the cooked lentils and sliced chestnuts in a pan together with the sauce. Add 1 cup stock and olive oil or butter. Bring to a boil and simmer for a few minutes. Taste, and add honey or vinegar if you wish. Serve the cooked lentils and chestnuts with a little olive oil or melted butter.

*Those who do not eat meat may rejoice in this and the following two "vegetarian" dishes.*

## Lentils and Leeks

*1 c. lentils*
*2½ c. water*
*2 heads of leeks, sliced*
*½ t. coriander*
*pinch each of fennel,*
*rosemary (or rue), and*
*pennyroyal if available*
*1 t. mint*
*1 t. wine vineger*
*1 T. honey*
*¼ c. vegetable stock*
*¼ c. boiled white wine*
*2 T. olive oil or butter*
*flour*
*ground pepper*

Cook lentils in water, and partially drain, retaining about a ½ cup of liquid in the pot. Add sliced heads of leeks.

In a mortar, grind coriander seeds, fennel, rosemary (or rue), pennyroyal, and mint. Moisten spices with vinegar. Blend with honey, vegetable stock, and boiled wine. Pour this sauce over the cooked lentils. Bring to a boil, stirring from time to time, and simmer till leeks are tender. Taste, and add honey or vinegar if necessary. Thicken with flour if you wish. Moisten with a few drops of olive oil or butter, sprinkle with pepper, and serve.

*This dish is excellent when stir-fried with green peppers, celery, mushrooms, broccoli and carrots.*

## Peas with Leeks in Basil Wine Sauce

*1 lb. fresh, shelled peas*
*½ c. water*
*2 heads of leeks, chopped*
*½ t. coriander*
*¼ t. cumin*
*½ t. ground pepper*
*½ t. celery seed (or lovage)*
*pinch each of caraway and*
*aniseed*
*¼ t. basil*
*½ c. chicken or veal stock*
*¼ c. white wine*

Steam peas in a little water, boil, and reserve liquid in pan when they are done. To this add finely chopped leeks. In a mortar, grind coriander, cumin, pepper, celery seed (or lovage), a pinch of caraway, aniseed, and basil. Blend with stock and white wine. Add this sauce to the peas and leeks, and cook gently over low heat in a covered pan for 25 minutes, stirring from time to time.

*The provocative taste of basil unites with the remaining herbs to enliven the otherwise bland flavor of the peas and leeks.*

## *Baked Peas with Meats Casserole*

*2½ c. fresh, shelled peas*
*olive oil or butter*
*1 lb. ham or pork belly, diced*
*½ c. stock*
*2 heads of leeks, chopped*
*1 t. coriander*
*½ c. Chicken Forcemeats (see p. 12)*
*½ c. cooked chicken breast, sliced*
*¼ lb. calf's brains*
*2 c. chicken stock*
*½ lb. Lucanian Spiced Sausage (see p. 15)*
*1 c. pine nuts or chopped almonds*

*First sauce:*
*1 t. ground pepper*
*1 T. celery seed (or lovage)*
*1–1½ t. oregano*
*½ t. ginger*
*casings*

*Second Sauce:*
*2 hard-boiled egg whites*
*dash of white pepper*
*¼ c. finely chopped almonds*
*1 T. honey*
*1 c. white wine*
*2½ c. chicken or veal stock*

Cook, then drain peas, and moisten with a little olive oil or butter. Set aside. Dice ham or pork, and put in a pan with ½ cup stock, leeks, and coriander. Simmer 30 minutes on top of stove. Set aside. Put forcemeats, chicken breast, and calf's brains in a pan, cover with stock, and cook till done. Set aside. Cook sausages and set aside. Roast nuts in the oven a few minutes.

To make the first sauce, in a mortar, grind pepper, celery seed (or lovage), oregano, and ginger. Moisten with ¼ cup liquid from the pork pan. Heat to a boil, and set aside.

Now take a deep, straight-sided (for turning upside-down) oiled casserole dish, and line it with casings. Grease with a little olive oil, then sprinkle the bottom of the dish with the nuts, seasoned with a little sauce. Cover with a layer of peas, then a second layer of diced ham, leeks, and sliced sausage. Sprinkle with sauce, and add a layer of peas. Cover with forcemeats and finish with a final layer of peas and sauce. Cook, uncovered, for 40 minutes in a 325°F oven (or cook over low heat).

Meanwhile, make the second sauce with finely minced egg whites, white pepper, almonds, honey, white wine, and stock. Blend and bring to a boil. Simmer for 25 minutes to reduce.

Carefully turn the cooked peas casserole onto a platter. Take off the casings and pour the sauce over the pressed peas. Serve.

*This is one of Apicius' most demanding dishes, and well worth the effort. To save time I prepare a number of* Lucanian Spiced Sausages *and freeze them.*

## Peas Indigo with Squid in Wine

2 c. fresh, shelled peas
2 heads of leeks, chopped
½ t. coriander
1 c. squid or small cuttlefish (Sepiola rondoletti)
1 T. olive oil
½ c. fish stock
¼ c. white wine
1 T. chives, finely chopped

Cook the peas, drain, leaving ½ cup liquid, and reserve the rest for sauce. Then add leeks and coriander. Simmer 15 minutes. Meanwhile cover cleaned
cuttlefish or squid with water, and cook in their ink
till tender. While they are cooking add the olive oil,
fish stock, white wine, chives, and coriander.

*The unusual color makes a memorable meal. Very
good served with a chilled, dry white wine.*

Sauce:
1 t. coriander
½ t. ground pepper
½ t. celery seed (or lovage)
¼ t. oregano
pinch of caraway
½ c. peas stock
¼ c. white wine
¼ c. sweet raisin wine or
muscatel
ground pepper

To make a sauce, grind the coriander, pepper, celery
seed (or lovage), oregano, and caraway. Add to the
stock reserved from the peas. Combine with white
and sweet wines. Bring the sauce to a boil, simmer
to reduce, and keep hot.

Now drain the cooked cuttlefish, chop very finely,
and add them to the peas in their liquid. Cook together for a few minutes, drain, and serve in the hot
sauce with a sprinkling of pepper.

## Chilled Peas Vinaigrette

2 c. shelled, fresh peas
1 medium onion, finely
chopped
2 hard-boiled egg whites
3 T. olive oil
1 T. cider vinegar
(1 soft-boiled egg yolk)

Steam peas, drain, and immerse in cold water.
When the peas are cold, drain, and toss to remove
liquid.

Into a mixing bowl, chop onion very finely. Add
chopped egg whites, fresh olive oil, and vinegar.
Pour the chilled peas into a serving dish. (If desired,
add the yolk of a soft-boiled egg to the peas.) Season
with the vinaigrette sauce, and serve.

*I often serve* Chilled Peas Vinaigrette *as the vegetable to balance a richly spiced meat dish, such as* Rabbit
Stuffed with Liver and Sausage.

## *Peas or Beans with Meat Dumplings*

*2 c. shelled, fresh peas or green beans*
*cooked beef or pork dumplings*

First, cook the vegetables and reserve stock.

Prepare dumplings using the recipe for *Seasoned Chicken Forcemeat Dumplings* (see p. 12), replacing the fowl meats with an equal amount of pork or beef.

*Sauce:*
*½ t. cumin*
*pinch of rosemary (or rue)*
*½ t. celery seed*
*2 t. honey*
*½ c. vegetable stock*
*¼ c. boiled white wine*
*2 t. olive oil*
*¼ c. white wine*
*ground pepper*

For the sauce, grind together in a mortar, cumin, rosemary (or rue), and celery seed. Mix with the honey, stock, boiled wine, olive oil, and wine. Bring this sauce to a boil, then stir into the dish of peas or beans. Add cooked beef or pork dumplings. Serve with a sprinkling of pepper.

## Peas or Beans in Parthian Fennel Sauce

*2 c. shelled, fresh peas or green beans*

Steam the peas or beans till tender, and reserve stock.

*Sauce:*
*½ t. fennel*
*½ c. vegetable stock*
*¼ c. boiled white wine*
*olive oil*

Make a sauce with the fennel, stock, and boiled white wine. Bring to a boil, then simmer for 25 minutes to reduce. Combine the peas with the sauce. Sprinkle with olive oil and serve.

## Peas with Sausage and Calf's Brains

*½ lb. sliced calf's brains (or deboned chicken breast)*
*¼ lb. Lucanian Spiced Sausage, sliced (see p. 15)*
*½ c. chicken livers and giblets*
*½ c. chicken or veal stock*
*2 t. olive oil*
*2 heads of leek, sliced*
*1 t. coriander*
*2 c. shelled, fresh peas*

In a casserole, put sliced brains or chicken slices. Add sliced sausage, chicken livers and giblets, stock, olive oil, leeks, and ground coriander. Braise, covered, for one hour in a 325°F oven. Meanwhile, steam the peas, and reserve stock.

*Sauce:*
*1 t. ground pepper*
*1 t. celery seed (or lovage)*
*½ c. vegetable stock*
*¼ c. white wine*
*2 t. olive oil*

For the sauce, first grind together pepper and celery seed (or lovage). Blend with stock, white wine, and olive oil, heat and bring to a boil, then simmer 15 minutes to reduce. Turn the cooked peas onto a serving dish. Cover with the braised meats, and season with the sauce.

## *Peas or Beans Vitellian with Leeks and Fennel*

*2 c. shelled, fresh peas or green beans*
*water*
*2 leeks, thinly sliced*
*1 t. coriander*
*5 grape or small cabbage leaves*

Steam peas or beans for 15 minutes, and reserve stock. Now add leeks, coriander, and grape or cabbage leaves. Simmer gently for 10 minutes more.

*Sauce:*
*½ t. ground pepper*
*1 t. celery seed (or lovage)*
*1 t. oregano*
*pinch of fennel seeds*
*½ c. vegetable stock*
*¼ c. white wine*
*olive oil or butter*

Meanwhile, in a mortar, grind pepper, celery seed (or lovage), oregano, and a pinch of fennel seeds. Combine with stock and wine. Bring to a boil, then simmer slowly for 20 minutes to reduce. Pour the sauce over the vegetables, stirring from time to time. Sprinkle with fresh olive oil or melted butter, and serve.

## *Beans in the Pod in Coriander Sauce*

*1 lb. fresh, unshelled beans*

Steam beans for 10 minutes. Drain.

*Sauce:*
*¼ t. ground pepper*
*½ t. celery seed (or lovage)*
*¼ t. cumin*
*1 t. coriander*
*1 c. chicken or veal stock*
*½ c. white wine*
*1 T. olive oil or butter*

In a mortar, grind together pepper, celery seed (or lovage), cumin, and coriander. Blend with stock and white wine. Pour this sauce over the beans, and add olive oil or butter. Simmer together gently, stirring, until the beans are fully cooked and the flavors mingled.

*This dish makes an excellent accompaniment to most roasted meats or fowls.*

## Beans Apicius with Sausage and Dumplings

*1 lb. fresh, unshelled beans*
*½ c. Lucanian sausage, sliced*
*½ c. cooked pork forcemeat dumplings*
*½ c. cooked chicken breast, sliced*
*½ c. cooked pork shoulder, diced*
*1 t. ground pepper*
*1 t. celery seed (or lovage)*
*1 t. oregano*
*pinch of aniseed*
*1 t. coriander*
*2 t. finely chopped onion*
*½ c. white wine*
*1 c. meat stock*
*2 t. olive oil or butter*

Put beans into a clay (or other) cooking pot. Prepare dumplings using the recipe for *Seasoned Chicken Forcemeat Dumplings* (see p. 12), replacing the fowl meats with an equal amount of pork. Add the sliced sausage (see p. 15), pork dumplings, chicken breast, and pork shoulder. Then, in a mortar, grind pepper, celery seed (or lovage), oregano, aniseed, and coriander. Blend with onion, and white wine. Pour the mixture over the beans and meats in the pot, and add stock and olive oil or butter. Stir together, cover, and simmer gently until beans are tender.

*The combination of flavors is richly satisfying. Very good served with boiled potatoes, and a red wine.*

## Beans and Leeks in a Simple Sauce

*1 lb. fresh unshelled beans*
*1 t. coriander*
*3 leeks, sliced*
*1½ c. water*

In a pan, combine beans with leeks and coriander. Add water, and bring to a boil, then simmer over low heat for 30 minutes. After 15 minutes, continue to cook in the following sauce.

*Sauce:*
*½ t. ground pepper*
*1 t. celery seed (or lovage)*
*1 t. oregano*
*¼ t. thyme*
*rosemary (or rue)*
*½ c. chicken or veal stock*
*1 T. olive oil or butter*
*ground pepper*

For the sauce, in a mortar, grind together pepper, celery seed (or lovage), oregano, thyme, and rosemary (or rue). Blend with the stock. Fifteen minutes before they are cooked, pour the sauce over the vegetables. Add olive oil or butter. Continue to simmer over low heat until the vegetables are done, stirring from time to time. Serve, with a sprinkling of pepper.

*This pleasant dish is particularly good with roast chicken or duck.*

## *Commodus' Beans with Aniseed and Eggs*

| | |
|---|---|
| *1 lb. fresh, unshelled beans* | Put beans in a pan with water, cook lightly, drain, |
| *½ c. water* | and reserve liquid. |

*Sauce:*
*1 t. ground pepper*
*½ t. celery seed (or lovage)*
*pinch of ground aniseed*
*2 t. chopped onion*
*½ c. chicken or veal stock*
*½ c. white wine*
*3 raw egg yolks*

For the sauce, in a mortar, grind pepper, celery seed (or lovage), and aniseed. Moisten with a tablespoon of liquid from the beans. Combine with onions, stock, white wine, and well beaten egg yolks. Pour over the drained beans. Transfer everything to a casserole, and cook gently in a 325°F oven until the dish is firm. Serve.

*Named after the mad emperor, Commodus, this superb recipe for beans was no doubt invented by his chef.*

## *Beans and Chicken Quiche with Cumin*

*1 chicken*
*½ c. chicken stock*
*½ c. white wine*
*2 t. olive oil*
*2 small onions, finely chopped*
*1 t. coriander*
*(½ lb. calf's brains)*
*1 lb. fresh, unshelled green beans*
*1 t. cumin*
*pepper, to taste*
*1 t. coriander*
*3 raw eggs*
*1 c. stock*
*pine nuts or chopped almonds*

Cut chicken into pieces. Cook for 30 to 40 minutes in a sauce made with the stock, white wine, and olive oil, together with one chopped onion, coriander (and parboiled calf's brains, if you wish). When done, drain, reserve stock, and bone the chicken pieces.

Cook the beans in water, without any seasonings, drain, and reserve liquid. Sprinkle one chopped onion, and coriander over the beans. Take a casserole, butter it, and arrange the beans in alternate layers with the chicken pieces (and chopped brains).

Next, in a mortar, grind pepper and cumin. Mix with stock from the pan of meat. Add well beaten eggs and combine with liquid from the cooked beans. Pour over the casserole. Decorate with pine nuts or chopped almonds. Cook gently in a 350° F oven for 30 minutes, and serve when firm.

*A serving of this quiche with a lettuce salad makes a splendid lunch.*

## Chicken or Suckling Pig Stuffed with Green Beans

4 lb. roasting chicken
1½ c. fresh, unshelled
green beans
½ c. calf's brains (or lamb
½ c. calf's brains
½ c. Lucanian Spiced
Sausage (see p. 15), pork
sausage, or blood sausage

Sauce:
1 t. pepper or 1 T. roughly
ground peppercorns
¼ t. celery seed (or lovage)
½ t. oregano
½ t. ginger
½ c. chicken or beef stock
1 T. sweet raisin wine or
muscatel
¼ c. white wine
casing
flour
white pepper

Prepare the sauce by grinding pepper, celery seeds (or lovage), ginger, and oregano in a mortar. Mix these with the stock, sweet wine, and white wine. Bring to a boil, then simmer the sauce for 15 minutes.

Next, stuff the chicken with layers of beans, alternating with chopped brains and sliced sausage. Pour a little of the sauce into each of the layers. Skewer and tie the bird with string, and put in a roasting pan. Roast for 30 minutes in a 400°F oven, then lower temperature to 300°F and cook for 1 to 1½ hours.

Serve with a gravy made from the pan drippings thickened with flour, using additional chicken stock as needed, and sprinkle with white pepper.

*The stuffing is incredibly rich, and the mingling of flavors is almost exotic. This dish needs very little for company—possibly a green salad, a hot roll, and a glass of red wine. But your guests will be feeding their eyes as you carve.*

## Green Beans in Coriander Sauce

2 c. green beans
1 c. bean stock
1½ t. coriander
1 T. butter
½ t. cumin
1 T. chives, chopped

Steam green beans for 10 minutes or until tender. Make a sauce with stock from the steaming pan, coriander, and cumin. Bring to a boil, then simmer over low heat for 25 minutes to reduce. Add to the beans and reheat. Serve with butter and a garnish of chives.

*This dish is a good complement to many of the fowl and roast dishes, and enlivens the fish dishes in* THE FISHERMAN, BOOK 10.

## Green Beans in Mustard Sauce

*2 c. green beans*

Steam the green beans in a little water till tender, and partially drain.

*Sauce:*
*½ t. mustard seed*
*pinch of rosemary (or rue)*
*¼ t. cumin; 2 t. honey*
*¼ c. pine nuts or almonds 1*
*t. wine vinegar*
*¾ c. beef stock*

To prepare the mustard sauce, grind together mustard seed, rosemary (or rue), and cumin. Add to honey, finely chopped nuts, vinegar, and stock. Heat the sauce, then pour it into the pan of cooked green beans. Stir and simmer for a few minutes. Serve with butter and a sprinkling of pepper.

## Beans with Celery and Leeks

*2 c. choice green beans*

Steam green beans until tender, drain, and reserve liquid.

*Sauce:*
*1 t. ground rosemary*
*1 c. celery, chopped*
*2 heads of leeks, chopped*
*1 t. wine vinegar*
*2 t. olive oil or butter*
*½ c. bean or vegetable stock*
*¼ c. boiled white wine*

Meanwhile, mix rosemary (or a pinch of rue), celery, and chopped leeks, vinegar, olive oil or butter, stock, and boiled wine. Bring to a boil, then simmer gently for 25 minutes to reduce. Pour over cooked green beans, and serve.

## Kidney Beans or Chick-peas in Fennel Sauce

*½ c. kidney beans or chick-peas*
*⅛ c. vegetable stock*
*⅛ c. white wine*
*¼ t. ground pepper*
*1 T. fennel*
*2–3 hard-boiled eggs*

Prepare beans ahead of time as in preceding recipe, then make the following sauce.

Combine stock with wine, pepper, and fennel, and bring to a boil. Simmer for 5 minutes over low heat, then combine with cooked beans, reheat, and serve. Drain and serve with sliced hard-boiled eggs.

Alternatively, pre-cook, drain, chill, and season in a cold sauce made with stock, white wine, pepper, and fennel. Decorate with hard-boiled eggs.

# Birds

## Roast Duck in Spiced Gravy

*3 lb. duck*
*3 c. water*
*¼ t. aniseed*
*water*
*2 T. butter or olive oil*
*1 c. duck stock*
*1 t. oregano*
*1 T. coriander*
*½ c. boiled wine*

To prepare the duck, simmer it for 30 minutes in water seasoned with aniseed. Remove the bird from the pot, reserving the stock, put it in a roasting pan, and season with a mixture of butter or olive oil, stock, oregano, and coriander. (At this point, an "Apician" stuffing may be added, made of sausage, damsons or dates, almonds, and spices.) Roast in a 375°F oven for 1½ hours, basting from time to time. For the last 30 minutes add the boiled red wine to the pan.

*Sauce:*
*½ t. ground pepper*
*1 t. celery seed (or lovage)*
*½ t. cumin*
*¼ t. coriander*
*pinch of fennel*
*½ t. rosemary (or a pinch of rue)*
*½ c. boiled wine*
*dash of wine vinegar*
*1 c. gravy from roasting pan*
*flour*

To make the sauce, grind pepper, celery seed (or lovage), cumin, coriander, fennel, and rosemary (or rue) in a mortar. Add to boiled wine (see p. 3), vinegar, and gravy from the roasting pan. Bring the sauce to a boil, simmer to blend flavors, and thicken with flour. Serve the duck on a platter with the sauce.

*Very good served with carrots, and cauliflower, or with broccoli in a cheese sauce.*

## Plum Sauce for Roast Duck and Chicken

½ t. ground pepper
2 t. chopped onion
1 T. lovage (or celery seed)
1 t. cumin
½ t. celery seed
½ c. damsons (or plums)
¼ c. mead or 1 T. honey
2 c. chicken stock
dash of wine vinegar
½ c. boiled wine
1 T. olive oil or butter

In a mortar, grind together pepper, onion, lovage (or celery seed), cumin, and celery seed. Add chopped damsons. Blend with mead or honey, stock, vinegar, boiled wine, and olive oil or butter. Bring to a boil and simmer for 30 minutes over very low heat. Serve with the roasted duck or chicken.

*This delectably pungent sauce is good with other meats as well.*

## Roast Duck in a Blanket of Turnips

3 lb. duck

¼ t. aniseed
3 turnips, cooked
1 T. olive oil or butter
1 c. turnip stock
1 T. chives, chopped
1 T. coriander
⅓ c. sweet red wine or port
1 c. bread crumbs
½ c. thinly sliced head of leek
1 t. coriander

Sauce:
¼ t. each pepper & cumin
½ t. coriander
pinch of fennel
1 t. wine vinegar
1 c. pan gravy

Simmer the duck in water seasoned with aniseed for 30 minutes. Meanwhile, cook the turnips in water, drain them, and save the liquid from the pot. Put the bird in a roasting pan and season with a mixture of butter or olive oil, turnip stock, chives, and coriander.

For a stuffing to complement the bird, mix bread crumbs with leek and coriander. Mash the cooked turnips to a pulp and spread in a blanket over the duck. Roast, uncovered, in a 375°F oven for 1½ hours. One hour before serving, add sweet wine or port with which to baste the roast. Finish in the following sauce.

To make the sauce, in a mortar, grind together pepper, cumin, coriander, and fennel. Add to vinegar and gravy from the roasting pan. Pour this sauce over the bird and the turnips, and cook together for the last 15 minutes. Thicken the gravy with flour, and serve with a sprinkling of pepper.

## Nut Sauce for Braised Duck

½ t. ground pepper
1 t. celery seed (or lovage)
½ t. cumin
1 t. coriander
1 t. mint
½ t. oregano
⅛ c. pine nuts or almonds
⅛ c. dates
2 c. duck or chicken stock
1 T. olive oil or butter
1 T. honey
½ t. mustard seed
½ c. red wine

In a mortar, grind together pepper, celery seed (or lovage), cumin, coriander, mint, and oregano. Add finely chopped nuts and chopped dates. Combine with stock, olive oil or butter, honey, mustard seed, and wine. Bring to a boil, then simmer for 25 minutes to reduce. Pour over the braised duck and serve.

*Rich flavors combine superbly with the texture of chopped nuts in this delicious sauce.*

## Zucchini Sauce for Roast Duck

½ t. ground pepper
½ t. celery seed (or lovage)
½ t. oregano
2 c. chicken stock
1 c. pan gravy
1 T. honey
dash of wine vinegar
2 t. olive oil
flour
1 medium zucchini, ½ acorn or butternut squash, or 2 c. broad beans
1 c. chicken livers
ground pepper

This sauce is to be poured over the duck 20 minutes before the bird is done.

First, in a mortar, grind pepper, celery seed (or lovage), and oregano. Combine with stock and gravy from the roasting pan. Add honey, vinegar, and olive oil or butter. Bring this sauce to a boil and thicken with flour. Add parboiled, sliced zucchini, squash, or lightly cooked broad beans. Pour over the duck and finish cooking. (Add lightly sautéed, chopped chicken livers, if you wish.) Serve the bird in the sauce, and sprinkle with finely ground pepper.

*As zucchinis grow so prolifically, it is always satisfying to find interesting new uses for them.*

## Date Sauce for Braised Duck

½ t. ground pepper
1 t. lovage (or celery seed)
1 t. celery seed
pinch of mustard seed (or rocket seed)
1 t. coriander
sprig of mint
¼ c. dates, finely chopped
1 T. honey
1 t. wine vinegar
1 c. chicken stock
½ c. boiled red wine
pinch of mustard seed

In a mortar, grind together pepper, lovage (or celery seed), celery seed, mustard (or rocket seed), coriander, and mint. Add to chopped dates. Combine with honey, vinegar, stock, boiled wine, and mustard seeds. Bring to a boil, simmer to blend flavors, and pour over the roasting duck 20 minutes before it is done.

Alternatively, braise the bird in the sauce from the beginning, correcting seasonings 20 minutes before the duck is done.

## Raisin Sauce for Partridge

½ t. ground pepper
1 t. celery seed (or lovage)
½ t. celery seed
sprig of mint
1 t. ground peppercorns (or myrtle berries)
¼ c. dark raisins
1 T. honey
½ c. red wine
1 c. chicken stock

In a mortar, grind together pepper, celery seed (or lovage), celery seed, mint, and peppercorns (or myrtle berries). Add to raisins. Mix with honey, red wine, and stock. Bring to a boil and simmer for 20 minutes before serving.

Alternatively, the bird may be braised in this sauce.

## Rosemary Sauce for Partridge and Game Birds

½ t. ground pepper
½ t. celery seed (or lovage)
sprig of mint
1 t. rosemary (or rue seed)
1 c. chicken stock
½ c. white wine
1 T. olive oil or butter

In a mortar, grind together pepper, celery seed (or lovage), mint, and rosemary (or rue) seed. Add stock, white wine, and olive oil or butter. Braise the bird in this mixture until done.

Or roast the bird and serve it in the rosemary sauce.

# Book Six

## OF BOILED PARTRIDGE,
## HAZEL HEN, AND TURTLEDOVE

[UNTITLED] [*Sauce for Partridge*] [Combine] pepper, lovage, celery seed, mint, myrtle berries or raisins, honey, wine, vinegar, stock, and olive oil. Serve chilled.

[UNTITLED] [*Partridge*] Boil the partridge in its feathers, and then pluck the bird while it is still wet. It is possible to cook a newly slaughtered bird in the sauce [described above], so that the flesh does not harden. If the partridge was killed [three or more] days previously, it should be boiled [first and the sauce added afterwards].

IN PERDICE ET ATTAGENA ET IN TURTURE  [*Sauce*] *for Partridge, Hazel Hen, and Turtledove*  [Mix] pepper, lovage, mint, and rue seed. Add stock, unmixed wine, and olive oil. Heat.

> *Ringdoves delay then quench the loins:*
> *He who'd lust shouldn't eat this bird.*
>
> Martial.

## OF WOOD PIGEONS AND DOVES

IN ASSIS  [*Sauce*] *for Roasted* [*Wood Pigeons and Doves*]  [Use a sauce made from these ingredients:] pepper, lovage, coriander, caraway, dried onion, mint, egg yolks, dates, honey, vinegar, stock, olive oil, and wine.

ALITER ELIXIS  [*Sauce*] *for Boiled* [*Wood Pigeons and Doves*]  [In a mortar, bruise] pepper, caraway, celery seed, and parsley. Add country sauce, dates, honey, vinegar, wine, olive oil, and mustard.

ALITER  [*Sauce for Wood Pigeons and Doves*]  Use pepper, lovage, parsley, celery seed, rue, nuts, dates, honey, vinegar, stock, mustard, and a little olive oil.

ALITER  [*Sauce for Wood Pigeons and Doves*]  [Grind] pepper, lovage, and fresh laser. Add [a little] stock and wine. [Simmer.] Pour over the dove or wood pigeon. Sprinkle with pepper and serve.

## Sweet Onion Sauce for Roast Game Birds

½ t. ground pepper
½ t. celery seed (or lovage)
½ t. coriander
pinch of caraway
sprig of mint
2 t. chopped onion
¼ c. dates, finely chopped
1 t. honey
dash of wine vinegar
1 c. chicken stock
2 t. olive oil or butter
½ c. white wine
2 raw egg yolks

In a mortar, grind together pepper, celery seed (or lovage), coriander, caraway, and mint. Add to onion and chopped dates. Blend with honey, vinegar, stock (including pan drippings), olive oil or butter, and wine. Heat, then thicken with well beaten egg yolks. Pour over the roasting birds, and cook together for the last 20 minutes.

Or pour the sauce over the cooked birds and serve.

*This wonderful sauce is good with any fowl.*

## Parsley-Mint Sauce for Braised Game Birds

½ t. ground pepper
pinch of caraway
½ t. celery seed
2 t. parsley
¼ c. Country Mint Sauce
(see p. 6)
¼ c. dates
1 t. honey
dash of wine vinegar
½ c. white wine
2 t. olive oil or butter
pinch of mustard seed
1 c. chicken stock with
pan drippings

Cook the birds as you would duck (see p. 81), and braise in this sauce until done. Or roast the parboiled birds and serve them in the sauce.

In a mortar, grind pepper, caraway, and celery seed. Add to parsley, Country Mint Sauce, and chopped dates. Combine with honey, vinegar, wine, olive oil or butter, mustard seed, and stock. Bring to a boil, then gently simmer for 25 minutes to reduce before serving.

*I like this sauce with pigeons, and served with brown rice.*

## Sweet Basting Sauce for Game Birds

½ t. ground pepper
1 t. lovage (or celery seed)
2 T. parsley
½ t. celery seed
½ t. rosemary (or rue)
¼ c. dates, finely chopped
1 t. honey
dash of wine vinegar
½ t. mustard seed
2 t. olive oil or butter
1 c. chicken stock with
pan drippings

In a 325°F oven, half cook the birds for 45 minutes in a roasting pan with olive oil or butter, then finish in the sauce, basting occasionally.

In a mortar, grind together pepper, lovage (or celery seed), parsley, celery seed, and rosemary (or rue). Add finely chopped dates. Combine with honey, vinegar, mustard seed, olive oil or butter, and stock. Bring to a boil, then add to the roasting pan.

*This and the following sauces are all very good with chicken.*

## Simple Basting Sauce for Game Birds

½ t. ground pepper
¼ t. celery seed (or lovage)
½ t. ginger
¾ c. chicken stock
½ c. white wine

In a mortar, grind pepper, celery seed (or lovage), and ginger. Add to stock and wine and stir together. For the last 45 minutes, pour over the roasting birds and cook together, uncovered, in a 325°F oven, basting from time to time.

## Spiced Sweet Wine Sauce for Birds and Fowl

½ t. ground pepper
½ t. cumin
1 t. savory
1 t. celery seed (or lovage)
1 t. mint
¼ c. raisins, damsons, or plums
3 t. honey
½ c. red wine (or myrtle wine)
1 t. wine vinegar
1 c. chicken stock
1 t. olive oil or butter
1 celery stalk

In a mortar, grind pepper, cumin, savory, celery seed (or lovage), and mint. Add to raisins or finely chopped plums. Blend with honey, red wine, vinegar, stock, and olive oil or butter. Bring to a boil, simmer gently for 25 minutes to reduce, stirring with a stalk of celery.

## Saffron Nut Sauce for Birds and Fowl

*½ t. ground pepper*
*1 t. parsley*
*1 t. celery seed (or lovage)*
*½ t. mint*
*pinch of saffron*
*½ c. white wine*
*¼ c. hazelnuts or almonds,*
*grated*
*1 T. honey*
*1 t. wine vinegar*
*1 c. chicken stock*
*1 t. olive oil or butter*
*1 celery stalk*
*sprig of fresh mint*

In a mortar, grind together pepper, parsley, celery seed (or lovage), mint, and a pinch of saffron. Combine with wine. Add roasted grated hazelnuts or almonds, honey, wine, vinegar, and stock. Put olive oil or butter in a pan, heat and add the sauce. Bring to a boil and simmer for 25 minutes over low heat to reduce. Stir with celery and a sprig of mint.

Score the skin of a nearly roasted bird and pour this sauce over it. Cook together for a few minutes in the oven and serve.

## Cumin Nut Sauce for Braised Game Birds

*½ t. ground pepper*
*½ t. lovage (or celery seed)*
*½ t. cumin*
*½ t. celery seed*
*⅓ c. hazelnuts or almonds,*
*grated*
*1 T. honey*
*2 c. chicken stock*
*1 t. wine vinegar*
*2 t. olive oil or butter*

In a mortar, grind together pepper, lovage (or celery seed), cumin, and celery seed. Add grated hazelnuts or almonds, honey, stock, vinegar, and olive oil or butter. Bring to a boil, then simmer for 25 minutes to reduce.

## Green Herb Sauce for Game Birds

½ t. ground pepper
pinch of caraway
¼ t. cumin
pinch of spikenard, if
available
pinch of bay leaf
fresh herbs to taste (thyme,
oregano, lovage, or
celery leaf)
¼ c. dates, finely chopped
1 t. wine vinegar
¼ c. white wine
¾ c. chicken stock
2 t. olive oil or butter

In a mortar, grind together pepper, caraway, cumin, spikenard, and bay leaf. Add the green herbs tied in a cheesecloth, finely chopped dates, vinegar, wine, stock, and olive oil or butter. Bring to a boil, then simmer gently for 20 minutes to reduce. Remove herbs and serve.

*If your "game" is a chicken netted at the supermarket, use a lot of oregano, at least a teaspoonful. Lovage or celery leaves can also be used to decorate the bird before you carve. Very good with boiled potatoes, with sprigs of parsley and a garnish of raw mushrooms.*

## Sweet and Sour Sauce for Roast Goose

10 lb. goose

Sauce:
1 t. ground pepper
¼ t. caraway
1 t. cumin
1 t. celery seed
½ t. thyme
½ t. ginger
¼ c. hazelnuts or almonds
1 T. honey
1 T. wine vinegar
1 c. chicken stock
2 t. olive oil or butter

To release the fat, parboil the goose in a pan half covered with water. Then roast the goose slowly in a 350° F oven for 3 to 3½ hours. One hour before it is done, add this sweet and sour sauce, and baste with it from time to time.

In a mortar, grind together pepper, caraway, cumin, celery seed, thyme, and ginger. Add to ground or very finely chopped hazelnuts or almonds. Blend with honey, vinegar, stock, and olive oil or butter. Bring to a boil, then simmer over low heat for 20 minutes to reduce.

## Seasonings for Cooking "High" Poultry

½ t. aniseed
1 t. ground pepper
½ t. celery seed (or lovage)
1 t. thyme
1 t. mint
¼ c. hazelnuts or almonds
¼ c. chopped dates
1 T. honey
1 T. wine vinegar
½ c. white wine
2 c. chicken stock
2 t. olive oil or butter

First put the no longer fresh bird in a pot, with water seasoned with aniseed. Cook for 30 minutes. Now transfer the prepared bird to a roasting pan and add a blended mixture of these strong seasonings: pepper, celery seed (or lovage), thyme, mint, finely chopped nuts and dates, honey, vinegar, wine, stock, and olive oil or butter. Heat this mixture to a boil, then add to the roasting pan. Baste from time to time until done.

*Do not think it is necessary to age your bird to use this excellent recipe, though in Apicius' time such a sauce helped improve "high" poultry.*

## Sesame Seed Sauce for Roast Goose

½ t. ground pepper
1 t. celery seed (or lovage)
1 t. toasted sesame seeds
1 t. parsley
1 t. mint
1 t. dried onion
1 t. honey
½ c. white wine
1 c. chicken stock
1 t. wine vinegar
2 t. olive oil or butter

In a mortar, grind together pepper, celery seed (or lovage), sesame seeds, parsley, mint, and dried onion. Blend with honey, white wine, stock, vinegar, and olive oil or butter. Bring to a boil and simmer gently for 25 minutes to reduce. Or cook together with the roast bird for the last 25 minutes.

## Hot Braised Goose Served with Cold Sauce Apicius

*1 medium braised goose*

*Sauce:*
*½ t. ground pepper*
*¼ t. celery seed (or lovage)*
*½ t. coriander*
*pinch of rosemary (or rue)*
*1 c. defatted goose or chicken
stock*
*2 t. olive oil*

After cooking, take the goose out of the pot and blot it dry.

For the sauce, in a mortar, grind pepper, celery seed (or lovage), coriander, mint, and rosemary. Mix with stock and olive oil. Then bring to a boil and simmer gently for 10 minutes. Chill. Serve with the hot goose.

## Pungent Ginger Dressing for Braised Chicken

*¼ t. aniseed*
*1 t. mint*
*½ t. ginger*
*1 T. wine vinegar*
*1 date, finely chopped*
*¼ c. chicken stock*
*¼ t. mustard seed*
*3 T. olive oil*
*½ c. boiled white wine*
*(see p. 3)*

To make this cold dressing for serving with braised chicken, first grind aniseed, mint, and ginger. Combine with vinegar, chopped date, chicken stock, mustard seed, olive oil, and boiled white wine.

*This sauce can also be used with green salads.*

## Aniseed Chicken

*4 lb. chicken*  Take the whole chicken and braise in water for approximately 20 minutes. Drain, reserve stock, and wipe dry.

*Sauce:*  For the sauce, combine aniseed, mint, ginger, vin-
*¼ t. aniseed*  egar, dates, stock, mustard, olive oil, boiled white
*1 t. mint*  wine, and honey. Heat to the boiling point and sim-
*½ t. ginger*  mer gently for 20 minutes.
*1 t. wine vinegar*  Now score the chicken's skin and pour aniseed
*3 dates, finely chopped*  sauce over it. Roast in a 300°F oven for 2 hours,
*1 c. chicken stock*  basting frequently with the liquid from the roasting
*¼ t. mustard seed*  pan. Sprinkle with mild pepper before serving.
*2 t. olive oil*
*½ c. boiled white wine (see*
*p. 3)*
*1 t. honey*
*ground pepper*

## Caraway-Ginger Chicken in a Clay Pot

*4 lb. chicken*  To make the sauce, combine pepper, celery seed
*Sauce:*  (or lovage), caraway, stock, white wine, and ginger
*1 t. pepper*  with hot water. Pour this sauce over the chicken,
*½ t. celery seed (or lovage)*  and cook in a covered clay pot till the bird is tender.
*¼ t. caraway*
*½ c. chicken stock*  *Here Apicius specified the use of a pot made of Cumae-*
*¼ c. white wine*  *an clay, but the important thing is to cook the chicken*
*½ t. ginger*  *slowly in a well used clay vessel.*
*½ c. hot water*

## Almond Sauce for Chicken or Guinea Hen

*3 lb. guinea hen or chicken*
*1 t. ginger*
*1 t. ground pepper*

Sprinkle ginger and pepper over the dressed guinea hen or chicken. Roast in a 350–400°F oven for 1 hour or till done.

*Sauce:*
*¼ t. ground pepper*
*½ t. cumin*
*½ t. coriander*
*pinch of fennel*
*pinch of rosemary (or rue)*
*¼ c. dates, finely chopped*
*¼ c. almonds or filberts, grated*
*1 t. wine vinegar*
*1 c. chicken stock*
*1 t. olive oil or butter*
*ground pepper*

For the sauce, grind pepper, cumin, coriander, fennel, and rosemary (or rue) in a mortar. Add to finely chopped dates, and grated almonds or filberts. Blend with vinegar, stock, and olive oil or butter. Bring the sauce to a boil and pour over the roast bird. Sprinkle with a little pepper, and serve.

*Delicious served with brown rice and a dish of mushrooms cooked lightly in a wine sauce.*

## Chicken with Ginger or Fennel

*4 lb. chicken*
*½ t. ground pepper*
*½ t. celery seed (or lovage)*
*1 t. ginger or ½ t. fennel*
*1 c. chicken stock*
*½ c. white wine*
*ground mild pepper*

Put prepared bird in a clay pot (or covered casserole). Grind pepper, celery seed, and ginger or fennel. Mix with stock and white wine. Cook chicken in a 375°F oven in sauce for 1½ hours, basting occasionally. Serve sprinkled with mild pepper.

*I prefer the ginger to the fennel. Serve with roast potatoes for a pleasant combination.*

## Ginger Marinade for Roast Chicken Pieces

*1 t. ginger*
*1 t. ground pepper*
*¼ c. olive oil*
*1 T. parsley*
*chicken stock*

Blend ground ginger, pepper, olive oil, stock to cover meat and parsley. Leave chicken parts in the marinade overnight, then bake, covered, at 400°F in a clay pot (or casserole) until done.

*This dish combines simplicity with elegance.*

### Chicken in Thyme Sauce

4 lb. cooked chicken
½ t. ground pepper
1 t. thyme
½ t. cumin
pinch of fennel
1 t. mint
pinch of rosemary (or rue)
1 t. wine vinegar
¼ c. dates, finely chopped
1 t. honey
2 c. chicken stock
2 t. olive oil or butter

To make the sauce, in a mortar, grind pepper, thyme, cumin, fennel, mint, and rosemary (or rue). Blend with vinegar, chopped dates, honey, stock, and olive oil. Bring to a boil, then simmer the cooked chicken for 30 minutes in this sauce before serving, basting occasionally.

*The flavors of chicken and thyme mingle very well, and in this sauce they are supported by a superb blend of seasonings. I enjoy chicken with a variety of accompaniments, but in this case* Alexandrine Squash *is particularly apt.*

### Chicken with Squash in Hot Thyme Sauce

Add 1 t. ground mustard to the thyme sauce described in the preceding recipe. Serve chicken and sauce together with cooked squash, vegetable marrow, zucchini, or pumpkin.

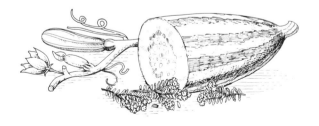

## *Chicken Vardanus with Chives and Hazelnuts*

*2 lbs. chicken parts*
*2 T. olive oil*

Take chicken parts and brown them in olive oil.

*First sauce:*
*1 c. chicken stock*
*2 t. olive oil or butter*
*½ c. white wine*
*1 T. fresh chives, chopped*
*1½ t. coriander*
*1½ t. savory or sage*

For the first sauce, mix stock, olive oil, white wine, chives, coriander, and savory or sage, according to taste. Cover, and cook the browned chicken parts in this sauce until done.

*Second sauce:*
*ground pepper, to taste*
*¼ c. hazelnuts or almonds, finely chopped*
*½ c. pan juices*
*1 c. milk*
*flour*

Now, in a mortar, grind pepper, mix with finely chopped nuts, and add to sauce from the chicken pan. Blend with the milk, pour over the cooked chicken, and bring to a boil. Thicken the sauce with flour. Add water to achieve desired consistency, and serve over the chicken pieces.

*The combination of chives and hazelnuts goes wonderfully well with slow cooked chicken breasts. Delectable served with hot rolls and* Alexandrine Squash.

## *Browned Chicken Frontinian*

*3 lb. chicken, cut into parts*
*2 T. olive oil or butter*

Brush chicken with olive oil or butter. Roast for 30 minutes in a 375°F oven to brown the meat. When done, finish in the following sauce.

*Sauce:*
*pinch of aniseed*
*½ t. savory*
*½ t. coriander*
*2 T. olive oil*
*1 c. chicken stock*
*1 T. chives*
*(½ c. white wine)*
*ground pepper*

To make the sauce, grind aniseed, savory, and coriander in a mortar. Combine with olive oil, stock, and chives. Put in a cooking pot with the browned chicken parts, and cook till done, basting from time to time with the sauce mixed with the chicken juices. (If you wish, add white wine to the mixture.) Serve the chicken in the sauce with a sprinkling of pepper.

*Very good served with steamed brown rice and sautéed mushrooms.*

## Chicken and Parsley Dumplings in Wine Sauce

2 lbs. chicken breasts
2 T. olive oil
1 medium onion, chopped
½ c. white wine
½ t. coriander
½ c. chicken stock
1 c. milk
2 T. honey
1 T. water

Dumplings:
1 t. parsley
½ c. all purpose flour
1 raw egg
milk

Sauté onion until soft, in olive oil. Now add the chicken breasts and continue cooking till they are brown. Add the white wine, coriander, and stock. Simmer for 40 minutes and set aside, putting the gravy into a fresh saucepan. To this, add milk, honey, and water, and keep warm over low heat.

Meanwhile, make 10 very small dumplings. First mix parsley with flour. Then put an egg in a measuring cup and add milk to fill ⅓ of the cup. Mix, then stir into the parsley and flour. Now heat the gravy-milk liquid until it boils, and add the dumpling mix by individual spoonfuls. Cover and simmer for 5 minutes, then uncover and simmer five more minutes.

Sauce:
¼ t. pepper
½ t. celery seed (or lovage)
1 t. oregano
1 t. honey
½ c. boiled wine (see p. 3)
1 c. chicken stock

For the sauce, grind together pepper, celery seed (or lovage), and oregano. Mix with honey, boiled wine, and stock. Bring to a boil, then simmer for 25 minutes to reduce. Pour the sauce over the reheated chicken and dumplings, and serve.

*After a winter's day pruning trees or splitting wood I particularly appreciate this hot, filling dish. It needs little else to make the meal except, perhaps, a pint mug of homemade beer. In fact, any cold day, whatever the season, is a good excuse to indulge in a healthy serving of* Chicken and Parsley Dumplings.

## Almond Ginger Stuffing for Chicken

*4 lb. chicken*
*½ t. ground pepper*
*¼ t. celery seed (or lovage)*
*2 t. ginger*
*½ lb. ground beef*
*½ c. boiled wheat berries*
*1 c. cooked calf's brains, chopped*
*3 raw egg yolks*
*½ c. chicken or beef stock*
*1 t. olive oil*
*whole peppercorns*
*½ c. almonds*

To make this stuffing for a roast chicken (or suckling pig), combine ground pepper, celery seed (or lovage), and ginger, with ground beef, boiled wheat, and chopped calf's brains. Bind with well beaten egg yolks. Add stock to moisten, olive oil, a few roughly ground peppercorns, and the almonds (whole or chopped, as you wish).

*You can add filberts chopped in half to the stuffing and substitute pure pork sausage meat for calf's brain. Delicious served with carrots fried in cumin and olive oil, and some white wine. Follow with ice cream and a dash of Cointreau for a festive dessert.*

## Stuffed Roast Chicken in White Sauce

*4 lb. chicken*

*Sauce:*
*2 T. butter*
*2 T. white pastry flour*
*1 c. milk*
*1 T. parsley*
*ground pepper*

Stuff the chicken with the *Almond Ginger Stuffing* in the preceding recipe and roast it in the oven.

To make the sauce, first melt butter over low heat in a saucepan. Combine with flour, gradually add milk, and simmer till thickened, stirring constantly. Stir in parsley and pour over the cooked fowl.

*Serve at once, with a sprinkling of pepper, your favorite green vegetables, and boiled potatoes.*

# Gourmet Recipes

## Tripe with Fennel Cream Sauce

*1 lb. sliced tripe*
*6 small onions*
*water*

Simmer the tripe with the halved onions and water for 4 hours in a covered pan. Drain, then finish cooking over low heat for 1 hour, with the onions, in the following cream sauce.

*Sauce:*
*2 T. butter*
*2 T. flour*
*1 c. milk*
*1 c. beef stock*
*1 t. wine vinegar*
*pinch of ground fennel*
*⅛ t. ground pepper*

For the sauce, first melt the butter over low heat. Slowly add flour, then the milk. Mix with the stock, vinegar, fennel, and pepper. Pour over the tripe and onions, and finish cooking till the tripe is done.

*Very satisfying served on a rainy winter's day with slices of bread and butter, and a pot of strong Orange Pekoe tea. To my taste, this is Apicius' best tripe recipe.*

## Tripe with Honey Ginger Sauce

*1 lb. sliced tripe*

*Sauce:*
*⅛ t. ground pepper*
*¼ t. ginger*
*1 t. celery seed*
*1 t. honey*
*1 t. wine vinegar*
*2 c. beef stock*
*1 t. mint*

Simmer the tripe for 4 hours in water, in a covered pan, and drain. Then finish cooking for 1 hour in the following sauce.

For the sauce, in a mortar, grind together pepper, ginger, and celery seed. Add to honey, vinegar, and beef stock. Pour over the tripe and cook gently together. Twenty minutes before serving, add mint.

## Tripe with Cinnamon-Nutmeg Sauce

*1 lb. sliced beef tripe* Simmer the tripe in a covered pan for 4 hours, then drain and finish cooking for 1 hour in the following spiced wine sauce.

*Sauce:* For the sauce, combine beef stock with white wine,
*½ c. beef stock* and spice the mixture with cinnamon and nutmeg.
*½ c. white wine* Pour over the tripe and cook gently together till the
*⅛ t. cinnamon* tripe is done. Sprinkle with pepper and serve.
*pinch of nutmeg*
*⅛ t. ground pepper*

## Seasonings for Spare Ribs, Cheeks, and Crackling

*ground pepper* Simmer meat for 2 hours in water seasoned to taste
*reduced pork stock* with pepper, reduced pork stock, and ginger.
*ginger* Alternatively, cook meat in water, and finish for 20 minutes in seasoned stock.
Serve in wine sauce. (See p. 3.)

## Pork Liver in Celery Wine Sauce

*1 lb. pork liver* Slice and sauté the liver in olive oil, and serve in a
*olive oil* reduced wine sauce.

*Sauce:* To make the sauce, in a mortar, grind together pep-
*½ t. pepper* per, thyme, and celery seed (or lovage). Combine
*½ t. thyme* with stock, red wine, and olive oil. Bring the sauce
*1 t. celery seed (or lovage)* to a boil, simmer to reduce for 20 minutes, and pour
*¾ c. pork or chicken stock* over the liver slices.
*¼ c. red wine* *Good for dinner with a dish of carrots and potatoes, or*
*1 t. olive oil* *for lunch with hot rolls and a glass of Bordeaux.*

## *Broiled Pork Liver with Bacon Slices*

*1 lb. pork liver*

*Marinade:*
*1 c. pork or chicken stock*
*½ t. ground pepper*
*1 t. celery seed (or lovage)*
*6 cloves (or laurel berries)*
*3–4 bacon slices*
*wine sauce*

Pound the liver and steep for 2 hours in a marinade of stock seasoned with pepper, celery seed (or lovage), and a few crushed cloves (or laurel berries). Wrap the marinated liver in bacon slices, and broil in oven.

*Serve with the reduced wine sauce from preceding recipe, or use straight from the oven for hors d'oeuvres.*

## *Marinated Pork Hors D'oeuvres*

*1 lb. choice pork or beef*

*Marinade:*
*1 t. ground pepper*
*1 t. celery seed (or lovage)*
*pinch of aniseed*
*1 t. cumin*
*½ t. ginger*
*5 cloves or laurel berries*
*pork or beef stock*

Cut meat into 1 inch cubes. In a mortar, grind pepper, celery seed (or lovage), aniseed, cumin, ginger, and a few cloves (or laurel berries). Blend with sufficient stock to cover meat. Put the meat into a dish and steep in the marinade overnight. Then drain and roast 1 hour in a 325°F oven.

*Sauce:*
*½ t. ground pepper*
*½ t. celery seed (or lovage)*
*1 c. pork or beef stock*
*sweet raisin wine or muscatel*
*flour*

For the sauce, grind together pepper and celery seed (or lovage). Add to stock, and sweeten with wine to taste. Bring to a boil and thicken with flour. Drench the hors d'oeuvres with this sauce and serve.

*I often serve Roman pork hors d'oeuvres at parties, with glasses of* Spiced Wine Apicius.

## MEAT HORS D'OEUVRES

OFELLAS OSTIENSES *Ostian\* Hors D'oeuvres* On the skin, mark out [bite-sized] pieces of choice meat, but leave the skin intact. Grind pepper, lovage, anise, cumin, silphium, and one laurel berry. Pour stock [over these seasonings and] blend. Pour [the mixture] into an angular vessel over the hors d'oeuvres. Steep. When the meat has reposed for two or three days in the marinade, bind it with twigs in the shape of a [Roman] ten, and put it in the oven. After cooking, separate the pieces of meat which you have marked out from each other. Grind pepper and lovage. Pour stock over these seasonings and add a little raisin wine for sweetness. Cook and then thicken the gravy with starch. Drench the hors d'oeuvres [with this sauce] and serve.

OFELLAS APICIANAS *Hors D'oeuvres Apicius* Remove the bones from pieces of meat. Roll into the shape of a wheel, binding them with twigs. Put in the oven. When it is browned, remove [from the oven] and, to expel moisture, dry the meat on a gridiron over a slow fire, taking care the meat does not scorch. [For the sauce, first] grind pepper, lovage, cyperus, and cumin. Blend with stock and raisin wine. Stir. Put the morsels of meat and the sauce into a saucepan. After cooking, remove the hors d'oeuvres from the pan and dry them. Serve them without sauce. Sprinkle with pepper and serve. If the meat should be fatty, remove the skin before the pieces are bound with twigs. In this way, also, it is possible to make these hors d'oeuvres from the belly of the animal.

OFELLAE APROGINEO MORE *Hors D'oeuvres in the Manner of Wild Boar* Steep [the pieces of meat] in [a marinade of] oil and stock. Seasoning is put into this when it is cooked. While it is on the fire, the [following] sauce is added and boiled again: ground pepper, green herbs, honey, and stock. Add starch when the sauce is boiling. Or, the morsels of meat may be simply boiled without [the marinade of] stock and olive oil, but sprinkled with pepper. Add the sauce described above and cook.

* Ostia was (and is) a seaport on the mouth of the Tiber River.

## Spiced Pork Hors D'oeuvres Apicius

*1 lb. choice pork (fillet, loin)*

*Sauce:*
*½ t. ground pepper*
*½ t. celery seed (or lovage)*
*pinch of ginger*
*¼ t. cumin*
*¾ c. pork or chicken stock*
*¼ c. raisin wine*
*ground pepper*

Cut meat in strips, roll, and secure with toothpicks (or twigs). Brown the pieces in a 300°F oven, and wipe away melted fat.

For the sauce, in a mortar, grind pepper, celery seed (or lovage), ginger, and cumin. Blend with stock and raisin wine. Slowly cook the meat in this sauce. When done, remove the hors d'oeuvres from the sauce and allow them to dry, or simmer till absorbed. Sprinkle each with a little pepper and serve.

*Warmly and pleasantly spiced, and so easy to make.*

## Pork Hors D'oeuvres with Green Herb Sauce

*1 lb. choice pork*

*Marinade:*
*2 t. olive oil*
*1 c. pork or chicken stock*
*1 t. thyme*
*2 t. celery seed (or lovage)*
*1 t. oregano*
*1 t. rosemary*

*Sauce:*
*¼ t. ground pepper*
*1 t. fresh mint, chopped*
*½ t. fresh thyme*
*½ t. fresh oregano*
*pinch of fresh rosemary*
*(or rue)*
*1 t. honey*
*1 c. pork or chicken stock*
*flour*

Cut the meat into 2 inch cubes. Steep the pieces for 8 hours in a marinade of olive oil and stock seasoned with thyme, celery seed (or lovage), oregano, and rosemary (or rue). Put the morsels in a braising pan and cook gently in the marinade for one hour.

Meanwhile prepare a sauce. Combine ground pepper, fresh herbs (chopped mint, thyme, oregano, rosemary or rue), honey, and stock. Bring the sauce to a boil, then thicken with flour. Serve the hors d'oeuvres in the sauce.

Alternatively, marinate the pieces of meat, then remove them from the marinade and cook with a sprinkling of pepper. Then finish cooking in the green herb sauce described above.

## Savory Pork or Beef Hors D'oeuvres

*1 lb. choice pork or beef*
*olive oil*
*1½ T. pork or beef stock*
*1½ T. water*
*1½ T. mild wine vinegar*
*1½ T. olive oil*

Cut the meat into thin 2-inch squares. Then sauté the morsels in olive oil until they are nearly done.

Next combine stock, water, vinegar, and olive oil. Pour into a cooking pot, and add the meats. Finish cooking over low heat, and serve.

## Tart Sauce for Roast Meats

*1 t. parsley*
*1 t. fennel*
*½ t. ginger*
*5 crushed laurel berries or peppercorns*
*½ t. basil*
*½ t. thyme*
*1 t. oregano*
*pinch of mint (or costmary)*
*½ t. chamomile (or pellitory)*
*1 t. celery seed*
*½ t. ground pepper*
*2 t. olive oil*
*1½ c. beef stock*

In a mortar, grind parsley, fennel, ginger, laurel berries or peppercorns, basil, thyme, oregano, mint, chamomile, celery seed, and ground pepper. Combine with olive oil and mix with stock. Bring to a boil, simmer for 15 minutes, then remove from heat and chill. Serve a little of the sauce with slices of cold roast beef.

Alternatively, add the mixture to the roasting pan, baste the meat, and serve the reduced sauce with the finished roast.

*You thought me cruel and greedy, Rusticus,*
*When I whipped the cook who burned our dinner.*
*If I unjustly beat him for a trifling offense,*
*Tell me, what worse crime can my cook commit?*

Martial.

## Roast Meats with Myrtle Wine Sauce

3 lb. pot or rump roast
water

Simmer the pot roast or rump roast in a covered pan with water for about 2 hours. Remove from the pot and reserve stock.

Sauce:
3–4 myrtle berries, cloves or juniper berries
½ t. cumin
½ t. ground pepper
1 T. honey
1 c. beef stock
¼ c. boiled red wine (see p. 3)
1 T. olive oil
(flour)
ground pepper

In a mortar, grind together cloves, myrtle or juniper berries, cumin, and pepper. Combine with honey, stock, boiled red wine, and olive oil. Bring to a boil, then roast meat for 1 hour, basting with the sauce, in a 325°F oven. Thicken sauce with flour, if you wish. Sprinkle roast with pepper and serve with the sauce.

## Roast Mutton with Thyme Sauce

3–4 lb. neck of mutton
2 c. water

Simmer the neck of mutton with water in a covered pan for a ½ hour and reserve liquid. Transfer meat to a roasting pan.

Sauce:
½ t. ground pepper
2 t. thyme
1 t. oregano
1 T. honey
2 c. mutton stock

To make the sauce, grind together pepper, thyme, and oregano. Combine with honey and stock. Pour over the mutton and roast in a 350°F oven for 2 hours or until done, basting with the sauce.

Alternatively, roast meat without the sauce, simmer sauce 25 minutes to reduce, and serve with finished roast.

## Rosemary-Ginger Sauce for Braised Meats

½ t. ground pepper
½ t. celery seed (or lovage)
½ t. oregano
½ t. rosemary (or rue)
pinch of ginger
1 T. chopped onion
¼ c. boiled wine
2 t. honey
½ t. cider or white vinegar
1 t. olive oil or butter
1 c. beef, pork, or
other meat stock
(flour)

In a mortar, grind pepper, celery seed (or lovage), oregano, rosemary (or rue), and ginger. Add chopped onion. Mix with boiled wine, honey, vinegar, olive oil, and stock. Heat, simmer to reduce for 25 minutes, and serve with cooked, drained meats. Or, the sauce can be thickened into a gravy with flour.

*This and the following thirteen recipes are for the very tender, choice cuts of beef and pork. While they have elements in common, each sauce is interestingly different. In each one, great care was taken by Apicius to enhance the natural flavors of fine meats by a subtle orchestration of the sauces' ingredients.*

## Onion Date Sauce for Braised Meats

½ t. coarsely ground pepper
2 T. chopped fresh parsley
1 c. beef, pork, or
other meat stock
1 t. cider or white vinegar
2 T. chopped dates
1 T. shallots or onions
1 t. olive oil or butter

Mix pepper, parsley, stock, vinegar, finely chopped dates and shallots, and olive oil or butter.

A ½ hour before meat is done, heat, then pour into the braising pan over the drained meats. Finish cooking the meats in the sauce, basting occasionally.

## Onion Fennel Sauce for Braised Meats

½ t. coarsely ground pepper
½ t. rosemary (or rue)
pinch of fennel
1 T. chopped onion
2 T. chopped dates
1 c. beef, pork, or
other meat stock
2 t. olive oil or butter

In a mortar, grind pepper, rosemary (or rue), and fennel. Add finely chopped onion and dates. Combine with stock and olive oil or butter.

A ½ hour before meat is done, drain the meat, then finish cooking and basting the drained meats in the sauce. Serve.

## Almond Wine Sauce for Braised Meats

½ t. ground pepper
1 c. beef, pork, or other
meat stock
¼ c. white wine
pinch of rosemary (or rue)
1 T. onion, finely chopped
¼ c. almonds or pine
nuts, finely chopped
1 c. spiced white wine (see
Spiced Wine Apicius, p. 4)
2 t. olive oil or butter
(flour)

Mix pepper, stock, white wine, rosemary (or rue), finely chopped onion and nuts, spiced wine, and olive oil or butter. Bring to a boil, then simmer for 25 minutes to reduce. Thicken with flour, if you wish. Serve the sauce with the cooked meats.

Or omit flour and finish cooking the lightly cooked (drained) meats in the sauce.

## Caraway-Oregano Sauce for Braised Meats

½ t. coarsely ground pepper
pinch of caraway or
aniseed
1 t. celery seed (or lovage)
½ t. thyme
½ t. oregano
2 T. chopped shallots or
onions
2 T. chopped dates
1 t. honey
1 t. cider or white vinegar
2 c. beef, pork, or
other meat stock
2 t. olive oil or butter

In a mortar, grind pepper, caraway or aniseed, celery seed (or lovage), thyme, and oregano. Add to finely chopped shallots and dates. Blend with honey, vinegar, stock, and olive oil or butter.

A ½ hour before meat is done, drain the meat, heat sauce and pour into the braising pan over the drained meats. Continue cooking to reduce sauce, and serve with meat.

## Damson Sauce for Braised Meats

½ t. coarsely ground pepper
½ t. cumin
1 t. celery seed (or lovage)
1 t. rosemary (or rue)
½ t. thyme
½ t. oregano
¼ c. damsons or plums
¼ c. white wine
¼ c. mead or 1 T. honey
1 t. cider vinegar or white
wine vinegar
1 c. beef, pork, or
other meat stock

In a mortar, grind together pepper, cumin, celery seed (or lovage), rosemary (or rue), thyme, and oregano. Add sliced plums. Blend with white wine, mead or honey, vinegar, and stock.

A ½ hour before meat is done, drain meat, heat sauce and pour it into the braising pan. Finish cooking meat in the sauce.

## Raisin Thyme Sauce for Braised Meats

¼ t. coarsly ground pepper
½ t. thyme
¼ t. cumin
1 t. celery seed
pinch of fennel
sprig of fresh mint
4–5 peppercorns (or juniper
or myrtle berries)
¼ c. raisins
¼ c. mead or 1 T. honey
1 c. beef, pork, or
other meat stock
savory, to taste

In a mortar, first grind together pepper, thyme, cumin, celery seed, fennel, and fresh mint. Add to peppercorns (or myrtle berries) and raisins. Combine with mead or honey and stock. Heat and stir in savory, to taste.

A ½ hour before meat is done, drain meat and pour sauce into pan with it. Finish cooking the meat in the sauce.

## Wine Egg Sauce for Braised Meats

½ t. coarsely ground pepper
1 t. celery seed (or lovage)
pinch of caraway
sprig of mint
1 t. bay leaf
1 t. spikenard (or bay leaves)
1 raw egg yolk
1 t. honey
¼ c. mead or
sweet white wine
1 t. white wine vinegar or
cider vinegar
2 t. beef, pork, or
other meat stock
2 t. olive oil or butter
small bouquet garni of
savory and chives
flour

Grind together pepper, celery seeds (or lovage), caraway, mint, bay leaf, and spikenard, if available. Blend with well beaten egg yolk, honey, mead or sweet wine, vinegar, stock, and olive oil or butter. Add savory and chives tied in cheesecloth.

A ½ hour before meat is done, drain meat and add sauce to it. Finish cooking in the sauce. Remove bouquet garni of savory and chives, and serve sauce with meat.

## Pepper Nut Sauce for Braised Meats

½ t. coarsely ground pepper
1 t. lovage (or celery seed)
¼ t. cumin
½ t. celery seed
½ t. thyme
¼ c. almonds, walnuts, pine,
or pistachio nuts
1 t. honey
1 t. white wine vinegar or
cider vinegar
1 c. beef, pork, or
other meat stock
2 t. olive oil or butter

In a mortar, grind together pepper, lovage (or celery seed), cumin, celery seed, and thyme. Add to finely chopped nuts. Blend with honey, vinegar, stock, and olive oil or butter.

A ½ hour before meat is done, drain the meat, add the sauce, and cook till done. Serve the meat with the sauce.

## Mustard Wine Sauce for Braised Meats

¼ t. ground pepper
½ t. celery seed
pinch of caraway
¼ t. savory
pinch of saffron
1 T. shallots or onion,
chopped
3 T. almonds, chopped
2 T. dates, chopped
1 c. beef, pork, or
other meat stock
2 t. olive oil or butter
pinch of ground mustard
½ c. white wine

In a mortar, grind together pepper, celery seed, caraway, savory, and saffron. Add finely chopped shallots or onions, almonds, and dates. Blend with stock, olive oil, and a little mustard. Heat and add wine.

A ½ hour before meat is done, drain the meat, and pour sauce over it. Finish cooking meat in the sauce and serve together.

## *Almond Parsley Sauce for Braised Meats*

½ t. coarsely ground pepper
½ t. ground pepper
½ t. celery seed (or lovage)
2 T. parsley
1 T. shallots or onions
¼ c. almonds, finely chopped
2 T. dates, chopped
1 t. honey
1 t. white wine vinegar or
cider vinegar
1 c. beef, pork, or
other meat stock
¼ c. white wine
2 t. olive oil or butter

In a mortar, grind together pepper, celery seed (or lovage), and parsley. Add chopped shallots or onions, almonds, and dates. Blend with honey, vinegar, stock, wine, and olive oil or butter.

A ½ hour before meat is done, drain the meat, and pour sauce over it. Finish cooking the meat in the sauce and serve together.

## *Peppercorn Leek Sauce for Braised Meats*

2 hard-boiled eggs, chopped
¼ t. pepper
1 t. cumin
1 T. parsley, chopped
¼ c. thinly sliced leeks
6 coarsely ground pepper-
corns (or myrtle berries)
1 T. honey
1 t. white wine vinegar or
cider vinegar
1½ c. beef, pork, or
other meat stock
2 t. olive oil or butter

Mix finely chopped hard-boiled eggs with pepper, cumin, and chopped parsley. Add leeks, and coarsely ground peppercorns (or myrtle berries). Combine with honey, vinegar, stock, and olive oil or butter.

A ½ hour before meat is done, drain the meat, and pour sauce over it. Finish cooking the meat in the sauce and serve together.

*How parsley thrives and gourds grow large*
*How endive loves to drink from streams*

Virgil.

IUS IN COPADIIS *Sauce for Choice Cuts* [Mix] pepper, celery seed, caraway, savory, saffron, shallots, roasted almonds, dates, stock, olive oil, and a little mustard. Add boiled wine to color [the sauce].

IUS IN COPADIIS *Sauce for Choice Cuts* [Mix] pepper, lovage, parsley, shallots, roasted almonds, dates, honey, vinegar, stock, boiled wine, and olive oil.

IUS IN COPADIIS *Sauce for Choice Cuts* [Mix] chopped hard-boiled eggs, pepper, cumin, parsley, cooked leek, myrtle berries, a goodly quantity of honey, vinegar, stock, and olive oil.

IUS IN ELIXAM ANETHATUM CRUDUM *Aniseed Marinade for Pork Delicacies* [Grind] pepper, aniseed, dried mint, and laser root. Pour vinegar [over these seasonings]. Add dates, honey, stock, and a little mustard. Blend with boiled new wine and with olive oil. Use this [marinade] also with neck of pork.

IUS IN ELIXAM ALLECATUM *Fish-pickle Sauce for Boiled Meats* [Mix] pepper, lovage, caraway, celery seed, thyme, shallots, dates, and strained fish-pickle. Blend these ingredients with honey and wine. Sprinkle chopped green celery over [the sauce]. Add oil and serve [with boiled meats].

## Aniseed Marinade for Braised Pork Tidbits

pork cubes
Marinade:
½ t. coarsely ground pepper
½ t. ground aniseed
sprig of mint
½ t. ginger
2 t. white wine vinegar or cider vinegar
¼ c. dates, finely chopped
2 t. honey
2 c. pork stock
1 t. ground mustard
½ c. boiled white wine (see p. 3)
2 t. olive oil

In a mortar, grind together pepper, aniseed, mint, and ginger. Moisten with vinegar. Add to finely chopped dates, honey, stock, and a little mustard. Stir in boiled wine and olive oil. Pour over the meat and leave in the marinade for at least six hours before cooking and serving.

This marinade is also good for braising sweetbreads.

(By reducing the aniseed to ¼ t., the wine to ¼ c., and stock to 1 c., an excellent sauce can be made with these marinade ingredients.)

## Fish-pickle Sauce for Braised Choice Meats

½ t. coarsely ground pepper
½ t. lovage (or celery seed)
pinch of caraway
½ t. celery seed
½ t. thyme
2 T. shallots or 1 T. onion, chopped
2 T. dates, chopped
1 T. fish-pickle (see p. 2)
1 t. honey
½ c. white wine
1 c. pork or beef stock
2 t. olive oil
chopped celery stalks
ground pepper

First, grind together pepper, lovage (or celery seed), caraway, celery seed, and thyme. Add to chopped shallots, dates, and fish-pickle. Blend with honey, wine, stock, and olive oil. Heat and add to drained, nearly cooked meats. Finish cooking meats in sauce until the liquid has been reduced by half.

Serve meats in the sauce, each portion garnished with finely chopped celery and sprinkled with freshly ground pepper.

## Roast Kidneys for One or Two

*1 pair veal, lamb, or*
*pork kidneys*
*¼ t. ground pepper*
*¼ c. roasted almonds, finely*
*chopped*
*½ t. coriander*
*pinch of fennel*
*2 T. olive oil*
*2 t. meat stock*
*fish-pickle (see p. 2)*
*bacon*

Remove the fat from the kidneys and discard. Cut kidneys lengthwise without separating them, into two parts. Spread them, and season with pepper, almonds, coriander, fennel, olive oil, and stock, or fish-pickle, if on hand. Close the kidneys and secure with toothpicks. Wrap in rashers of bacon, and roast in a 350° oven for about 35 minutes.

*This makes a surprisingly filling lunch, and is extremely tasty. Try to use sweet bacon free of added "smoke." A couple of hot rolls, and a tomato or two complete the meal.*

## Baked Ham

*4–5 lb. ham*
*1 c. figs*
*3 laurel or bay leaves*
*½ c. liquid honey*

*Pastry:*
*2½ c. flour*
*½ t. baking powder*
*1 c. shortening*
*1 raw egg*
*water*
*½ t. cider vinegar or*
*lemon juice*

Place the ham in a pan and half cover with cold water. Bring to a boil and simmer for 1 hour, then drain and discard the water. Add figs, laurel or bay leaves, and fresh water. Simmer for a further 45 minutes. Take ham from the pot, cool it, and remove the skin. Score ham deeply, and drench the incisions with liquid honey.

Make the pastry as directed below, roll it out and pull it around the ham. Smooth the ends for a more pleasing appearance.

Bake in a 350°F oven for 15 minutes or until pastry browns.

For the pastry, mix flour and baking powder. Cut the shortening into the mixture. In a bowl, beat the egg and add sufficient water to it to make ¾ cup of liquid. Add vinegar or lemon juice. Blend wet and dry ingredients with a fork, then cool the dough in the refrigerator for 1 hour before using it with the ham.

*My first experience of Apicius' cuisine was at the house of the late professor Edith Wightman. We feasted on baked ham, and drank spiced Roman wine in her garden on a mid-summer's evening until late into the night. The coat of pastry kept the ham sweet and fragrant.*

## "Must" Cake for Roast Pork

*Must cake:*
*2 c. white flour*
*3 t. baking powder*
*½ c. shortening*
*½ c. honey*
*2 raw eggs*
*1 c. cottage cheese*
*¼ t. aniseed*
*¼ t. cumin*
*bay leaves*
*¼ c. white grape juice or must*

Sift together flour, baking powder, aniseed, and cumin. Combine shortening, eggs, and honey. Combine dry ingredients with cottage cheese and then with other wet ingredients. Lastly, stir in the grape juice. Pour the batter into a greased and floured loaf pan. Decorate with bay leaves and bake in a 350°F oven for 40 minutes or until done.

*Pepper sauce:*
*½ c. sweet raisin wine or muscatel*
*½ c. grape juice or new wine*
*pinch of rosemary, rue, or sage*
*½ t. ground pepper*

To make pepper sauce, combine, raisin wine or muscatel, grape juice, a pinch of rosemary, rue or sage, and pepper. Bring to a boil, and simmer to blend flavors.

*Serve a roast shoulder or leg of pork in the pepper sauce, with slices of sauce-saturated must cake.*

## Bacon with Dill

*8 thick rashers of Canadian bacon*
*½ c. water*
*½ t. dill*

In a frying pan, barely cover bacon with water seasoned with dill. Fry the bacon, but do not allow it to become crisp. If desired, serve with a sprinkling of olive oil and salt to taste.

## Marinated Liver of Kid or Lamb

*1 lb. lamb, pork, calf, or goat liver*
*½ c. milk*
*1 raw egg*
*¼ c. water*
*2 T. honey*
*2 T. olive oil*
*½ c. boiled red wine (see p. 3)*
*ground pepper*

If necessary, remove membrane from liver, and with a knife make a few superficial incisions. Prepare a sweet marinade with milk, well beaten egg, and water mixed with honey. Immerse the scored liver in the marinade and steep for 6 hours.

Into a hot frying pan, pour olive oil. Add the prepared liver slices, and turn to brown both sides. Add the wine and simmer for 3 minutes on each side. Serve with a sprinkling of pepper.

## Lungs Apicius

*1 pair lamb's lungs*
*2 c. beef or chicken stock*
*2 raw eggs*
*1 t. honey*
*olive oil or butter*

Wash the lungs and cut in strips, removing the larger arteries. Place in a pot with stock, bring to a boil, and simmer for 2 hours. Drain, and combine with well beaten eggs and honey. Next, sauté lightly in olive oil or butter. Remove from the pan and place in a casserole with the following sauce.

*Casserole sauce:*
*½ t. ground pepper*
*¾ c. beef or chicken stock*
*1 t. thyme*
*1 t. celery seed (or lovage)*
*1 t. oregano*
*1 medium onion, chopped*
*¼ c. red wine or grape juice*

To make the sauce, grind together thyme, celery seed (or lovage), and oregano. Combine with onion, stock and wine or juice. Cook covered in a 300°F oven for 2 hours, and serve.

*My butcher sells this light delicacy by weight, which results in an exciting yet extremely inexpensive Roman dinner. Many people are hesitant to eat lungs, but they are very good indeed. Prepared in this way, the lungs taste much like kidneys.*

## HOMEMADE SWEETS AND HONEYED CHEESES

❡The paucity of recipes for Roman pastries and desserts in Apicius' *Cookery* does not accurately reflect their significance in the cookery of the ancient world. The recipes for these, along with culinary medicine and wine making, are in my opinion in the books missing from *The Roman Cookery of Apicius* as it has come down to us. Their existence can be inferred from a multitude of scattered sources in Greek and Roman history and literature.

DULCIA DOMESTICA *Homemade Sweets* Take palms or dates, with the stones removed, and stuff them with nuts or nut kernels and ground pepper. Salt the dates on top and bottom and fry in cooked honey, and serve.

❡In the preparation of sweets, Apicius used the word "pepper" loosely. In the first century A.D., cinnamon and nutmeg were thought by the Romans to have common points of origin with pepper. They were, in those days, prohibitively expensive.

ALITER DULCIA *Sweets* Strip off pieces of the best African must cake and immerse them in milk. When they have drunk [up all the milk they can, form them into small cakes]. Bake them in the oven, but not for long lest they become too dry. [After baking] remove [from the oven and] pour honey over the cakes while they are still hot. Puncture them so that they may drink [up the honey]. Sprinkle with pepper and serve.

> *Arise: even now boys are buying their morning*
> *pastries*
> *And the roosters of the dawn are everywhere alive*
> *with calls.*
>
> Martial.

## Dates Alexandrine

20 (whole) dates
20 blanched almonds
1 t. cinnamon
butter
liquid honey

Remove pits from dates. Roll almonds in cinnamon and stuff one in each date. Place dates on a greased pan, then coat each one with honey. Glaze in a 450°F oven for 10 minutes, then serve.

Dates Alexandrine *are a great favorite with the children in my first grade class, and with adults whenever they are served as hors d'oeuvres.*

## Sweet "Roman Toast"

white bread
milk
olive oil or butter
liquid honey

Remove the crusts from the bread, and slice it. Dip in milk and sauté in olive oil or butter. Sprinkle honey on top and serve.

*This recipe omits the egg customarily added with "French" toast, but is delicious nonetheless.*

## "Peppered" or Cinnamon Sweet Cakes

1¼ c. pastry flour
1 t. baking powder
½ t. ground rosemary (or rue)
⅓ c. almonds, chopped
1 t. cinnamon
¼ c. sweet raisin wine or muscatel
¼ c. grape juice or new wine
2 T. honey or brown sugar
milk
filberts (or hazelnuts)

Mix flour with baking powder. Blend with rosemary (or rue), almonds, and cinnamon. In a measuring cup combine sweet wine with grape juice (or new wine) and honey. Add milk to make 1 cup of liquid. Mix with the dry ingredients and bake in a 9-inch round pan, in a 375°F oven for 30 minutes. Garnish with roasted chopped nuts and serve.

For a rich variation, lightly spread liquid honey over the warm cake, and decorate with chopped nuts. Then prick the surface here and there with a fork and drizzle 2–3 T. of wine into the cake.

*If spread with honey this simple cake achieves a glossy elegance. It is very good made with wholewheat flour.*

## Rich Sweet Cakes

2 t. cinnamon
½ c. almonds, chopped
½ t. ground rosemary (or rue)
2 c. pastry flour
2 t. baking powder
¼ c. sweet raisin wine or muscatel
1 egg
4 T. honey or brown sugar
¾ c. milk
filberts or pecans

In a mixing bowl, put cinnamon, chopped almonds, and rosemary (or rue). Add flour, baking powder, and mix. Next, combine sweet wine, well beaten egg, honey, and milk. Blend and stir into the dry ingredients. Bake in a 375°F oven in a greased 9 inch round pan for 30 minutes. Pour a little honey on top of the finished cake and garnish with nuts.

*Apicius' inclusion of rue is daring, and only a pinch is needed. If unobtainable, rosemary can substitute. The hint of bitterness balances the flavor of the sweet ingredients and the nuts. Great fun at a tea party.*

## Roman Custard

2 c. milk
¼ c. honey or sugar
3 egg yolks
¼ t. nutmeg or cinnamon

To make the custard, first pour the milk into a bowl. Mix with honey and then scald in a saucepan. Remove from heat and add well beaten egg yolks. Add nutmeg or cinnamon and stir well. Pour into individual molds or into a baking dish. Bake uncovered at 325°F for 1 hour, or until set. Sprinkle with cinnamon or nutmeg, and serve.

## Honey Omelette

4 eggs
½ c. milk
4 T. butter or oil
2 T. liquid honey
cinnamon or nutmeg

Combine the eggs, milk, and butter. Butter a shallow pan, heat, and when the melted butter bubbles, pour in the eggs and cook the omelette. Do not fold. Serve with honey poured on top and a sprinkling of cinnamon or nutmeg. For a Roman mushroom omelette, add ¼ cup of mushrooms prepared as in *Sautéed Mushrooms*, p. 120.

*This is the origin of our modern omelette, a dish nearly as old as recorded history.*

## Fish-pickle Cheese Hors D'oeuvres

*1 c. mild white farmer's cheese*
*2 T. honey*
*2 T. mild fish-pickle (see p. 2)*
*1/2 t. ground pepper*

Coarsely grate the cheese, then combine with honey, fish-pickle, and coarsely ground pepper.

Alternatively, combine the grated cheese with 3 t. olive oil, 1 t. coriander, and 2 T. honey.

*Chill before serving as appetizers. Very good with thin, crisp breads. Delicious and easily made for parties, they mate wonderfully well with* Spiced Wine Apicius, *or dry white wines.*

## Onion Relish

*3–4 onions, chopped*
*2 T. olive oil*
*1/4 c. mild fish-pickle (see p. 2)*
*1 T. white wine vinegar or cider vinegar*
*1/4 t. cumin*

Mix the chopped onions with the olive oil, fish-pickle, vinegar, and cumin. Serve as a relish.

## Hot Onion Sauce

*4 onions, chopped*
*2 T. olive oil or butter*
*Sauce:*
*1/2 t. thyme*
*1/4 t. mint (or pennyroyal)*
*1/2 t. ground pepper*
*1 t. oregano*
*1 t. honey*
*2 t. white wine vinegar or cider vinegar*
*1/2 c. onion stock*
*1 T. fish-pickle (see p. 2)*

Strew the onions in a frying pan. Combine all the other ingredients and pour them over the onions. Heat and simmer for 5 minutes, or till onions are cooked.

*This is a hot sauce and a fitting complement to beef, lamb, goat, etc.*

## Wine Sauce for Mushrooms

*mushrooms*
*olive oil or butter*
*red wine*
*red wine vinegar*
*ground pepper*

Slice mushrooms and sauté in olive oil or butter. Combine red wine and vinegar (1 t. vinegar to ½ c. wine), add to mushrooms, and finish cooking them. Serve with a sprinkling of pepper.

*This simple wine sauce gives the mushrooms a deep, rich color and the flavor of red grapes. Serve with a multitude of meats.*

## Sautéed Mushrooms

*mushrooms*
*olive oil*
*red wine*
*coriander*

Sauté mushrooms in olive oil. Cook gently till done in red wine seasoned with ground coriander to taste.

*I serve these mushrooms with a number of meat dishes, particularly with pork and venison.*

## Mushrooms with Coriander

*mushrooms*
*¼ t. coriander to ½ c. boiled wine (see p. 3)*

Use a small saucepan and pour in just enough boiled wine to cover the mushrooms. For each half cup of wine use ¼ t. coriander. Cook mushrooms gently in the wine and coriander.

*In season, the use of green coriander corns lends éclat to this dish. It is marvelous served with roast or braised chicken, or duck.*

## Mushrooms with a Rich Sauce

*¼ lb. choice mushrooms*

*Sauce:*
*¼ t. ground pepper*
*½ t. celery seed (or lovage)*
*1 t. honey*
*2 T. mushroom liquid or stock*
*2 T. olive oil or butter*

Select choice mushrooms and slice them parallel to the stems. Cook them for three minutes in the following sauce.

For the sauce, grind together pepper and celery seed (or lovage). Combine with honey, mushroom liquid, and olive oil or butter. Bring to a boil, lower heat, and finish cooking with the mushrooms.

Alternatively, the mushrooms can be served raw with the hot sauce poured on top.

*Because of the exorbitant cost of truffles you may like to try these sauces with mushrooms.*

## Roasted Truffles in Wine

| | |
|---|---|
| *truffles* | Wash truffles, and brown them in the oven. Then |
| *1 c. veal stock* | slice and simmer for 5 minutes in a mixture of |
| *2 t. olive oil* | stock, olive oil, pepper, honey, and wine. Thicken |
| *¼ t. ground pepper* | the sauce with flour, and serve. |
| *1 t. honey* | Alternatively, after browning the truffles, punc- |
| *½ c. white wine* | ture them with a fork, then simmer 5 minutes in the |
| *flour* | sauce. |

## Lovage Sauce for Truffles

| | |
|---|---|
| *fresh truffles* | Grind together pepper, celery seed (or lovage), and |
| *Sauce:* | rosemary (or rue). Combine with stock, wine, and |
| *¼ t. ground pepper* | olive oil. Bring the sauce to a boil, then simmer |
| *½ t. celery seed (or lovage)* | together with sliced or punctured truffles for 5 min- |
| *¼ rosemary (or pinch of rue)* | utes, and serve. |
| *1 c. veal stock* | |
| *½ c. white wine* | |
| *2 t. olive oil* | |
| *flour* | |

## Rosemary Mint Sauce for Truffles

| | |
|---|---|
| *fresh truffles* | Combine pepper, fresh mint, rosemary (or rue), |
| *Sauce:* | with honey, olive oil, and wine. Bring to a boil, then |
| *¼ t. ground pepper* | simmer truffles in this sauce for 10 minutes, and |
| *sprig of mint* | serve. |
| *pinch of rosemary (or rue)* | |
| *1 t. honey* | |
| *1 T. olive oil* | |
| *½ c. white wine* | |

## Truffles with Leeks

*2 oz. truffles*
*3 heads of leeks*
*1 c. water*

Chop leeks into 1 inch segments and combine with washed, sliced truffles. Place in a pot with water and bring to a boil, then drain and reserve stock.

*Sauce:*
*¼ t. ground pepper*
*½ t. coriander*
*½ c. white wine*
*2 t. olive oil*

Meanwhile, combine pepper, coriander, and add stock from the pan. Stir in wine and olive oil. Bring this sauce to a boil, then add leeks and truffles to it, and simmer for 5 to 10 minutes more.

## Spiced Celery Sauce for Truffles

*a small quantity of fresh truffles*

Wash, then slice or puncture truffles with a fork.

*Sauce:*
*¼ t. ground pepper*
*pinch each of cumin, fennel, and rosemary (or rue)*
*sprig of mint*
*½ c. chopped celery*
*1 t. white wine vinegar or cider vinegar*
*½ c. white wine*
*dash of salt or 2 t. fish-pickle (see p. 2)*
*2 t. olive oil*
*1 c. vegetable stock*

For the sauce, grind together pepper, cumin, fennel, rosemary (or rue), and mint. Add celery, vinegar, wine, salt or fish-pickle, olive oil, and stock. Add to the truffles, bring to a boil, and simmer together for 5 minutes, then serve.

*To send presents of silver and gold*
*Or cloaks and togas*
*Is easy;*
*But giving some boleti...*
*That's hard.*

Martial.

## Sautéed Snails in Fennel Sauce

*12–15 snails*
*1 c. veal stock*
*pinch of fennel*
*¼ t. ground pepper*
*1 T. olive oil*

Remove the snails from their shells. Lightly sauté in olive oil seasoned with salt. Then cover with the following sauce and simmer till snails are done.

For the sauce, mix stock, fennel, pepper, and olive oil, and combine with snails.

## Snails Poached with Cumin

*12–15 snails*
*1 c. veal stock, or ½ c. white wine and ½ c. veal stock*
*¼ t. ground pepper*
*¼ t. cumin*

Remove the snails from their shells and place in a cookpot. Add stock and seasonings. Bring to a boil and simmer together till done.

## Eggs Poached in Wine Sauce

*4 chicken or duck eggs*
*2 T. chopped onion*
*1 c. red wine*
*¼ t. oregano*
*½ t. celery seed (or lovage)*
*ground pepper, to taste*

Grind together oregano, celery seed (or lovage), and pepper. Combine with onion and wine, and pour into a pan. Bring to a boil, then simmer. Carefully add eggs and poach according to taste.

*A deliciously subtle way to transform a familiar dish.*

## *Roman Scrambled Eggs*

*1 T. butter*
*4 eggs*
*3 T. chicken stock*
*3 T. white wine*
*⅛ t. fennel*
*ground pepper, to taste*

Melt butter in a pan. Combine eggs with chicken stock, wine, fennel, and pepper. Then pour into pan and scramble the mixture till done.

## *Sauce for Soft-boiled, Poached, or Scrambled Eggs*

*½ t. ground pepper*
*½ t. celery seed (or lovage)*
*1 T. finely chopped almonds*
*¼ c. mild fish-pickle (see p. 2)*
*1 t. honey*
*½ c. chicken stock*

Grind together pepper, celery seed, and almonds. Combine with fish-pickle, honey, and stock. Bring to a boil and serve with cooked eggs.

## EGGS

¶Eggs were customarily served at the "gustatio," or hors d'oeuvre courses at the beginning of a Roman dinner.

OVA FRIXA  *Fried Eggs*  [Fry them in] wine sauce.

*When a tide of white flows around saffron yolks,*
  *Season the eggs with the liquor of Spanish mackerel.*

Martial.

OVA ELIXA  *Boiled Eggs*  [Serve in a dressing of] stock, olive oil, and unmixed wine, or [season with] stock [mixed with] pepper and laser.

*When the young Julia Augusta was pregnant with Tiberius Caesar by Nero, she very much wanted to give birth to a boy and so she made use of a method of divination used by young women. She kept an egg warm in her bosom, and when she had to set it aside she consigned it to a nurse so that the warmth would not be interrupted... and nor was this method of divination false.*

Pliny.

IN OVIS HAPALIS  *Of Soft-boiled Eggs*  [Garnish with] pepper, lovage, soaked nut kernels, pine nuts, honey, vinegar, and stock.

# Quadrupeds

## Roast Pork with Cumin in Wine

*4–6 lb. boar or pork roast*

*Marinade:*
*water*
*1 t. myrtle berries, or juniper berries, or cloves*
*2 t. peppercorns*
*2 t. cumin*

*Sauce:*
*2 t. honey*
*½ c. chicken or pork stock*
*¼ c. red wine*
*½ t. ground pepper*
*roasting pan juices*

Wipe the roast dry. Immerse for 24 hours in a marinade of water, myrtle berries, peppercorns, and cumin. Roast uncovered in a 350°F oven for 30 minutes per pound.

To make the sauce, combine pepper, honey, stock, and pan juices. Bring to a boil and simmer for 30 minutes. Serve with the slices of meat.

Alternatively, braise the meat slowly in stock seasoned to taste with pepper. One hour before it is done, drain the pan, pour the sauce over the roast and finish cooking, spooning the sauce over the meat from time to time.

If you like, sprinkle additional cumin over the roast as it cooks.

*Though the original Latin specifies these recipes for wild boar, the Romans of Apicius' day were accustomed to eating "wild" boars which had been raised on farms.*

## Coriander Sauce for Pork, Beef, and Venison

*4–6 lbs. roast meat*

*Sauce:*
*½ t. ground pepper*
*2 t. celery seed (or lovage)*
*1 t. oregano*
*3–4 dried myrtle berries, or juniper berries, or cloves*
*1 t. green coriander*
*2 T. chopped onion*
*1 t. honey*
*1 c. pork or beef stock*
*½ c. red wine*
*1 T. olive oil or butter*

In a mortar, grind together pepper, celery seed (or lovage), oregano, dried myrtle berries, and coriander. Add chopped onion, to taste. Blend with honey, stock, red wine, and olive oil or butter. Bring to a boil and simmer for 30 minutes. Then pour over the roast meat slices.

Alternatively, finish cooking the roast in the sauce for ½ hour.

## Cumin Sauce for Roast Pork

4–6 lb. roast pork

Sauce:
1 t. coarsely ground
pepper (or more)
1 t. cumin
1 t. celery seed
½ t. chopped fresh mint
½ t. savory
pinch of saffron
¼ c. ground roasted pine
nuts or almonds
1 c. pork or beef stock
2 t. olive oil or butter

In a mortar, grind peppercorns and cumin. Add celery seed, chopped fresh mint, savory, saffron, and roasted pine nuts or almonds. Blend with stock and olive oil or butter. Bring the sauce to a boil, simmer for five minutes, pour over the roast, and serve.

*This elegant sauce achieves a fine balance between the strength of the pepper and cumin, and the delicacy of fresh mint, savory, and saffron. The ground nuts maintain the smooth consistency.*

## Hot Sauce for Roast Pork

4–6 lb. roast pork

Sauce:
½ t. coarsely ground pepper
1 t. lovage (or celery seed)
1 t. celery seed
1 t. chopped fresh mint
1 t. thyme
¼ c. grated or finely
chopped almonds
½ c. red wine
1 t. wine vinegar or
cider vinegar
1 c. pork or beef stock
2 t. olive oil or butter
2 T. chopped onion
½ t. rosemary (or rue)
(2 egg whites)

In a mortar, grind pepper, lovage, celery seed, chopped mint, thyme, and nuts. Blend with wine, vinegar, stock, and olive oil or butter. Add this sauce to the juices in the roasting pan, then add the chopped onion, and stir. Bring to a boil and simmer for 25 minutes, then serve with the roast meat.

For a richer texture, gradually add two egg whites to the sauce and stir gently. Serve with a sprinkling of pepper.

## Sweet Sauce for Roast Pork

*4–6 lb. roast pork*
*Sauce:*
*½ t. coarsely ground pepper*
*1–2 t. lovage (or celery seed)*
*½ t. cumin*
*⅛ t. fennel*
*1 t. oregano*
*⅛ c. pine nuts, almonds, or pistachio nuts*
*⅛ c. chopped dates (or sultanas)*
*2 t. honey*
*¼ t. mustard seed*
*1 t. wine or cider vinegar*
*1 c. pork or beef stock*
*2 t. olive oil or butter*

In a mortar, grind pepper, lovage (or celery seed), cumin, fennel, and oregano. Combine with finely chopped nuts, dates, honey, mustard seed, vinegar, stock, and olive oil or butter. Bring to a boil and simmer for 25 minutes, then serve with the cooked meat.

Alternatively, braise the meat in it for the last 25 minutes.

*This is a rich sauce for roast pork. You can rub the meat with cumin before cooking. Very good with steamed squash and roast potatoes.*

## Cold Sauce for Roast Pork or Ham

*4–6 lb. roast pork or ham*
*Sauce:*
*½ t. ground pepper*
*pinch of caraway*
*1 t. lovage (or celery seed)*
*1 t. coriander*
*pinch of aniseed*
*1 t. celery seed*
*½ t. thyme*
*¼ t. oregano*
*1 T. shallots or onions, chopped*
*1 t. honey*
*1 t. wine or cider vinegar*
*⅛ t. mustard seed*
*1 c. pork, chicken, or beef stock*
*2 t. olive oil or butter*

In a mortar, grind pepper, caraway, lovage, coriander, aniseed, celery seed, thyme, and oregano. Add to shallots or onions. Blend with honey, vinegar, mustard seed, stock, and olive oil or butter. Bring to a boil, then simmer for 25 minutes. Chill, and serve with slices of meat. Or serve hot, if you wish.

## Cold Wine Sauce for Roast Pork or Ham

*4–6 lb. roast pork or*
*ham*

*Sauce:*
*½ t. ground pepper*
*1 t. celery seed (or lovage)*
*½ t. cumin*
*½ t. thyme*
*½ t. oregano*
*pinch of fennel*
*⅛ t. mustard (or*
*colewort seed)*
*½ c. red wine*
*½ t. rosemary, and of rue, if*
*available*
*2 T. chopped onion*
*⅛ c. roasted hazelnuts or*
*almonds, finely chopped*
*⅛ c. dates, finely chopped*
*1 t. honey*
*1 t. wine vinegar or*
*cider vinegar*
*1 T. boiled red wine (see*
*p. 3)*
*1 c. pork or beef stock*
*2 t. olive oil or butter*

In a mortar, grind pepper, celery seed (or lovage), cumin, thyme, oregano, fennel, and mustard (or colewort) seed. Combine with wine, rosemary (and rue), onion, chopped nuts and dates. Blend with honey, vinegar, boiled wine, stock, and olive oil or butter. Bring to a boil, then simmer for 25 minutes. Chill, and serve with roast pork or ham. Or serve hot, if you wish.

*A wonderful cold lunch when served with pickles and homebaked bread in summer, with a glass of sparkling apple cider or chilled white wine.*

## Sweet Wine Sauce for Roast Pork

*4–6 lb. roast pork*

*Sauce:*
*½ t. ground pepper*
*1 t. lovage (or celery seed)*
*1 t. oregano*
*1 t. celery seed*
*½ t. cumin*
*pinch of fennel seed*
*½ t. rosemary (or rue)*
*1 c. pork or beef stock*
*¼ c. red wine*
*¼ c. sweet raisin wine or muscatel*
*flour*

In a mortar, grind pepper, lovage, oregano, celery seed, cumin, fennel seed, and rosemary (or rue). Blend with stock, red wine, and sweet wine. Bring the sauce to a boil, simmer to blend flavors, and thicken with flour. Coat the sides of the roast with the sauce, and serve.

Alternatively, baste the roasting meat in the sauce for the last hour of cooking, then thicken sauce, and serve.

## Ham in Terentine Sauce

*4 lb. ham with bone in*

*Sauce:*
*½ t. coarsely ground pepper*
*4–5 t. cloves (or juniper or laurel berries)*
*½ t. rosemary (or rue)*
*pinch of fennel*
*¼ c. pork or beef stock*
*¼ c. red wine*
*1 t. olive oil or butter*

Simmer ham for 1 hour in water, changing to fresh water after 30 minutes. Drain, cool meat, and separate skin from the flesh, leaving it attached at the small end. Score the ham, then season it with the reduced sauce below. Tie skin back in place with string, and bake in a 350°F oven for 2½ hours.

To make the sauce, grind together pepper, cloves or juniper berries, and rosemary (or rue). Add a pinch of fennel. Combine with stock, red wine, and olive oil or butter. Bring to a boil, simmer to reduce, and use as described above.

*Lean, dry venison can be wrapped in bacon or larded. Steaks are first browned in olive oil or butter, then finished in one of the savory sauces below. Cooked roasts may be served with the sauces.*

## Oregano Sauce for Venison Steaks or Roast

4 lbs. roast venison or steaks
Sauce:
¼ t. ground pepper
1 t. celery seed (or lovage)
pinch of caraway
½ t. oregano
¼ t. ginger
pinch of fennel seed
1 c. venison, beef, or chicken stock
¼ c. red wine
2 t. olive oil or butter
flour

In a mortar, grind pepper, celery seed (or lovage), caraway, oregano, ginger, and fennel seed. Blend with stock, wine, and olive oil or butter. Bring the sauce to a boil, then simmer slowly for 25 minutes to reduce, and serve over the cooked venison. Or thicken with flour and serve.

Alternatively, finish the venison steaks in the sauce for a few minutes before serving.

## Simple Sauce for Venison

4 lbs. roast venison or steaks
Sauce:
½ t. ground pepper
1 t. lovage (or celery seed)
pinch of caraway
1 t. celery seed
1 t. honey
1 t. wine vinegar or cider vinegar
1 c. venison, beef, or chicken stock
2 t. olive oil or butter
flour

In a mortar, grind peppercorns, lovage, caraway, and celery seed. Blend with honey, vinegar, venison stock, and olive oil or butter. Bring to a boil, then simmer slowly for 25 minutes, and serve with roast venison or with steaks.

Thicken sauce with flour, if you wish, before serving with meat.

## Nut Sauce for Venison

*4 lbs. roast venison or steaks*
*Sauce:*
*½ t. ground pepper*
*½ t. cumin*
*¼ c. onions or shallots, chopped*
*¼ t. oregano*
*⅛ c. roasted almonds, chopped*
*⅛ c. dates, chopped*
*1 t. honey*
*1 c. venison, beef, or chicken stock*
*¼ c. red wine*
*¼ t. mustard seed*
*1 t. wine or cider vinegar*
*2 t. olive oil or butter*

Combine pepper, cumin, chopped onions or shallots, and oregano. Add to finely chopped almonds and dates. Blend with honey, stock, wine, mustard seed, vinegar, and olive oil or butter. Bring to a boil, then simmer for 25 minutes. Serve with the cooked venison.

## Sweet Cumin Sauce for Venison

*4 lbs. roast venison or steaks*
*Sauce:*
*¼ t. ground pepper*
*½ t. cumin*
*¼ t. basil*
*¼ t. rue (or rosemary)*
*2 t. parsley*
*½ t. rosemary*
*½ t. mint*
*2 T. chopped onion*
*1 t. honey*
*1 c. venison, beef, or chicken stock*
*¼ c. sweet raisin wine or muscatel*
*2 t. olive oil or butter*
*flour*

In a mortar, grind pepper, cumin, rosemary, basil, parsley, rue (or rosemary), and mint. Blend with onion, honey, stock, sweet wine, and olive oil or butter. Bring the sauce to a boil, simmer for 25 minutes over low heat, and thicken with flour before serving with the cooked venison.

## Pine Nut Sauce for Venison

*4 lbs. roast venison or steaks*

*Sauce:*
*½ t. ground pepper*
*1 t. celery seed (or lovage)*
*2 t. parsley*
*1 t. cumin*
*¼ c. pine nuts or almonds, chopped*
*1 t. honey*
*1 t. wine or cider vinegar*
*½ c. red wine*
*2 t. olive oil or butter*
*1 c. venison, beef, or chicken stock*

In a mortar, grind pepper, celery seed (or lovage), parsley, and cumin. Add to nuts, then blend with honey, vinegar, wine, olive oil or butter, and stock. Bring to a boil, simmer for 25 minutes, then pour over cooked venison, and serve.

*Pine nuts were a favorite ingredient of classical cooks. In a sauce, they do not dominate like other nuts. With this dish, serve carrots and leeks for a pleasant balance.*

## Marinade for Venison Pot Roast

*4 lb. venison pot roast*

*Marinade:*
*1 t. ground pepper*
*1 t. crushed bay leaf*
*1 t. crushed spikenard (or bay leaf)*
*1 t. celery seed*
*1 medium onion, finely chopped*
*1 t. rosemary (or rue)*
*1 T. honey*
*2 T. sharp vinegar*
*3 dates, finely chopped*
*¼ c. raisins*
*1 T. olive oil*
*2 c. venison or beef stock*

Combine pepper, crushed bay leaf and spikenard, celery seed, chopped onion, rosemary (or rue), honey, vinegar, dates, raisins, olive oil, and stock. Marinate, covered, for 8 hours, basting occasionally.

Cook the pot roast in some of the marinade in a covered pot until done.

*If you like, add a half cup of Muscatel or another sweet wine to the marinade.*

## *Plum Sauce For Roast Venison*

*4 lbs. roast venison*
*Sauce:*
*½ t. ground pepper*
*1 t. lovage*
*2 t. parsley*
*¼ c. pitted plums, or*
*damsons (or prunes)*
*½ c. red wine*
*1 t. honey*
*1 t. wine vinegar or*
*cider vinegar*
*1 c. venison, beef, or*
*chicken stock*
*2 t. olive oil*
*1 T. chives*
*½ t. savory*

In a mortar, grind pepper, celery seed (or lovage), and parsley. Soak plums in wine, and combine with the herbs, honey, vinegar, stock, and olive oil or butter. Stir in the chives and savory. Bring the sauce to a boil, simmer and reduce for 25 minutes. Serve with the roast venison.

## *Mixed Spice Sauce for Venison Steaks or Cutlets*

*2 lbs. venison steaks or cutlets*
*Sauce:*
*¼ t. ground pepper*
*1 t. celery seed (or lovage)*
*pinch of caraway*
*½ t. cumin*
*2 t. parsley*
*½ t. rosemary (or rue)*
*1 t. honey*
*½ t. mustard seed*
*1 t. red wine vinegar*
*1 c. venison, beef or*
*chicken stock*
*2 t. olive oil*

In a mortar, grind pepper, celery seed (or lovage), caraway, cumin, parsley, and rosemary (or rue). Blend with honey, mustard seed, vinegar, stock, and olive oil or butter. Bring to a boil and simmer for 25 minutes to reduce. Pour over the cooked meat and serve.

## Thick Sauce for Venison Steaks or Cutlets

venison steaks or cutlets

Sauce:
¼ t. ground pepper
¼ t. rosemary
¼ t. basil
pinch of rue, if available
1 small chopped onion
1 t. honey
1 c. venison, beef, or
chicken stock
½ c. sweet raisin wine or
muscatel
2 t. olive oil
flour

Marinate the meat for 8 hours in the *Marinade for Venison Pot Roast*. Then cook the meat, pour the following sauce over it, and serve.

For the sauce, first grind together pepper, rosemary, basil (and rue). Add to onion. Blend with honey, stock, sweet wine, and olive oil. Bring the sauce to a boil, simmer for 25 minutes and thicken with flour before serving over the meat.

## Basil-Oregano Sauce for Venison Steaks or Cutlets

venison steaks or cutlets

Sauce:
¼ t. ground pepper
½ t. rosemary
¼ t. basil
2 t. parsley
1 t. oregano
pinch of rue, if available
1 c. venison, beef, or
chicken stock
1 t. honey
½ c. sweet raisin wine or
muscatel
2 t. olive oil
flour

In a mortar, grind pepper with rosemary, basil, parsley, oregano (and rue). Blend with stock, honey, sweet wine, and olive oil. Bring the sauce to a boil, simmer for 25 minutes to reduce, and thicken with flour before serving.

*Whether in a marinade or sauce, a sweet wine works best for venison. Outstanding with a recipe for sautéed mushrooms, and lightly steamed broccoli.*

### Hot Mint Sauce for Roast Mutton or Lamb

*3–4 lbs. roast mutton*

Roast the mutton and serve it with this sauce.

*Sauce:*
*dash of ground pepper*
*½ t. celery seed (or lovage)*
*⅛ t. cumin*
*3 sprigs fresh mint, (or heaped T. dried mint)*
*¼ t. oregano*
*pinch of thyme*
*pinch of fennel*
*¼ c. red wine*
*⅛ c. damsons or plums, finely chopped*
*2 T. honey*
*⅓ c. mild vinegar*
*olive oil*

For the sauce, first grind together pepper, celery seed (or lovage), cumin, finely chopped mint, oregano, thyme, and fennel. Moisten with a little red wine. Blend with damsons, honey, vinegar, and a few drops of olive oil. Bring to a boil, and simmer for 25 minutes. Serve with the roast mutton.

*Apicius specified wild sheep, but this sauce will work just as well with lamb chops or a leg of lamb from your local butcher.*

### Cold Sauce for Roast Mutton or Lamb

*3–4 lbs. roast mutton*

Roast the mutton and serve it with this cold sauce.

*Sauce:*
*¼ t. ground pepper*
*1 t. celery seed (or lovage)*
*½ t. thyme*
*⅛ t. cumin*
*¼ c. roasted pine nuts or almonds, finely chopped or grated*
*2 t. honey*
*1 t. vinegar*
*1 c. mutton or beef stock*
*2 t. olive oil*

Grind together pepper, celery seed (or lovage), thyme, and cumin. Add nuts, honey, vinegar, stock, and olive oil. Bring to a boil and simmer for 25 minutes. Use when it has cooled. Or serve hot, if you wish, with the roast meat.

*Though Apicius liked to serve this sauce cold, I prefer it hot. Very good with a dish of buttered peas, and roast potatoes.*

## Veal in Sweet and Sour Onion Sauce

*1 lb. ¾" veal steak*

*Sauce:*
*¼ t. ground pepper*
*1 t. lovage (or celery seed)*
*¼ t. celery seed*
*¼ t. cumin*
*½ t. oregano*
*1 medium onion,*
*finely chopped*
*2 T. raisins*
*1 t. honey*
*1 t. red wine vinegar*
*¼ c. red wine*
*2 t. olive oil*
*½ c. veal juices or beef stock*

Sauté the meat lightly in olive oil. Skim the fat from the frying pan, preserve juices, and finish cooking in the following sauce.

For the sauce, first grind together pepper, lovage (or celery seed), celery seed, cumin, and oregano. Add chopped onion, raisins, honey, vinegar, red wine, olive oil, and veal juices. Blend. Pour the sauce into the pan with the veal, cover, and cook very gently for 1 hour.

## Veal with Leeks, Apples, and Broad Beans

*1 lb. veal or stewing*
*beef, cubed*
*2 T. flour*
*1 t. ginger*
*½ t. ground pepper*
*2 T. olive oil*
*1 c. beef or vegetable stock*
*1 onion, chopped*
*1 c. leeks, chopped*
*3 medium cooking apples,*
*peeled and chopped*
*1 c. broad beans*
*ginger*
*mild ground pepper*

Roll 1-inch cubes of veal in flour, ginger, and pepper. Sear in olive oil. Put the browned meat in a covered baking dish and add stock. Cook in a 300°F oven for 40 minutes, then add onions, leeks, apples, and broad beans. Continue cooking for 40 minutes more or until beans are done.

Before serving, stir the apples into the liquid to make a thick sauce, and sprinkle a little more ginger or mild pepper over the dish.

*The Romans knew how to combine meats and fruits, although some of us have only tried pork with apple sauce. It is important to use only the freshest ingredients for this pleasant dish.*

## Caraway Sauce for Baked Veal

*1 lb. thick veal cutlets*
*olive oil or butter*
*½ t. ground pepper*
*½ c. beef stock or water*

Trim fat from the veal. Brown cutlets in olive oil or butter, then place in a covered baking dish. Add stock seasoned with pepper, and cook for 1 hour in a 325°F oven, or until done.

*Sauce:*
*½ t. ground pepper*
*1 t. lovage (or celery seed)*
*large pinch of caraway*
*1 t. celery seed*
*2 T. honey*
*dash of vinegar*
*1 c. veal or beef stock*
*2 t. olive oil or butter*
*flour*

For the sauce, grind together pepper, lovage, (or celery seed) caraway, and celery seed. Blend with honey, vinegar, stock, and olive oil. Heat the sauce, simmer slowly for 25 minutes, and then thicken with flour. Pour the sauce over slices of cooked veal and serve.

## Fennel Nut Sauce for Roast Veal or Cutlets

*1 lb. roast veal or cutlets*

Prepare veal as in preceding recipe.

*Sauce:*
*½ t. pepper*
*1 t. celery seed (or lovage)*
*large pinch of fennel*
*½ t. oregano*
*¼ c. almonds, chopped*
*¼ c. dates, chopped, or raisins*
*2 T. honey*
*2 c. veal or beef stock*
*½ t. mustard seed*
*2 t. butter*

In a mortar, grind pepper, celery seed (or lovage), fennel, and oregano. Add to chopped nuts and dates. Blend with honey, stock, mustard seed, and butter. Simmer for 25 minutes, and serve over slices of roast or sautéed meat.

*The Romans lived in England for centuries, so I think it is quite appropriate to serve Yorkshire pudding, and roast potatoes with Apicius' veal dishes!*

## OF KID AND LAMB

COPADIA HAEDINA SIVE AGNINA  *Choice Cuts of Kid or Lamb*
Cook them with pepper and stock. [Serve] with [a sauce of] sliced
green beans, stock, pepper, laser, fried cumin, pieces of bread, and a
little olive oil.

ALITER HAEDINAM SIVE AGNINAM EXCALDATAM  *Kid or
Lamb  Washed in Warm Water*  Put the choice cuts of meat into a
pan. Add onions, coriander chopped very finely, ground pepper, lovage, and cumin. Add stock, olive oil, and wine. Cook, transfer to a
stewing dish, and thicken [the gravy] with starch. [Serve.]

[ALITER HAEDINAM SIVE AGNINAM EXCALDATAM]  [*Kid or
Lamb Washed in Warm Water*]  Prepare the lamb's meat with the
ground seasonings in the mortar [written above], before cooking. Goat's
meat, however, should receive the ground seasonings during cooking.

HAEDUM SIVE AGNUM ASSUM  *Roast Kid or Lamb*  First cook
in stock and olive oil, [then remove from the pan and] score [the flesh].
Pour [a sauce of] pepper, laser, stock, and a little olive oil [over the
incisions]. Roast [the kid or lamb] on a gridiron. [When done] pour
[more of] the same sauce over the meat, sprinkle with pepper, and
serve.

ALITER HAEDUM SIVE AGNUM ASSUM  *Roast Kid or Lamb*
Use half an ounce of pepper, six scruples of wild spikenard, a little
ginger, six scruples of parsley, a little laser, half a pint of the best quality
stock, and one-eighth of a pint of olive oil.

*When lambs are fat and vines are mellow*
*Then shadows that deeply lie at the foot of mountains*
*Are soon to follow.*

Virgil.

## *Choice Cuts of Lamb or Kid in Thick Bean Sauce*

*2–3lbs. choice cuts of lamb or kid (leg, loin, rack)*
*1 t. ground pepper*
*1 c. beef or other meat stock*

Season meat with pepper, add stock, and roast in a 325°F oven for 2 hours or till done.

*Sauce:*
*1 c. sliced green beans*
*1 c. vegetable or beef stock*
*dash of ground pepper*
*1 t. ginger*
*¼ t. cumin*
*1 t. butter*
*½ c. bread bits or crumbs*

For the sauce, combine beans, stock, pepper to taste, ginger, and cumin, and simmer for 25 minutes over low heat. Before serving, add bread bits, and pour over slices of the cooked meat.

The bread crumbs serve the same function as would flour, to thicken the sauce. They seemed to be a culinary treat for Apicius.

## *Lamb or Kid in Coriander Onion Sauce*

*2–3 lbs. choice cuts of lamb or kid (leg, loin, rack)*
*1 medium onion, chopped*
*½ t. coriander*
*¼ t. celery seed (or lovage)*
*¼ t. cumin*

Season the meat with onion, coriander, celery seed (or lovage), and cumin. Roast, uncovered, in a 300°F oven for 2 hours. (After 1½ hours, add more spices to taste, if you wish.)

*Sauce:*
*½ t. coriander*
*¼ t. celery seed (or lovage)*
*¼ t. cumin*
*1 medium onion, chopped*
*2 c. vegetable or beef stock*
*2 t. butter*
*½ c. red wine*
*flour*

For the sauce, in a mortar, grind together coriander, celery seed (or lovage), and cumin. Add to onion, and combine with stock, butter, and wine. Bring to a boil and simmer slowly for 25 minutes. Thicken with flour and serve over the slices of meat.

*Wonderful served with freshly picked* Beans in the Pod in Coriander Sauce, *and, in season, new baby potatoes garnished with butter and parsley.*

## Roast Lamb or Kid in Ginger Sauce

*3–4 lb. lamb or kid roast*
*2 T. olive oil or butter*

*Sauce:*
*½ t. ground pepper*
*1 t. ginger*
*½ c. vegetable or beef stock*
*1 T. olive oil or butter*

Take the roast and moisten it with olive oil or butter. Roast uncovered for 1 hour at 325°F. Then score the roast lightly with a sharp knife, and over the incisions pour the sauce made with pepper, ginger, stock, and olive oil or butter. Continue roasting for 1 hour or till done, then serve with the same sauce.

## Parsley Sauce for Roast Lamb or Kid

*2–3 lb. lamb or kid roast*
*¼ t. ground pepper*
*1 small crushed bay leaf*
*1 t. parsley*
*½ t. ginger*
*1 c. vegetable or beef stock*
*2 t. butter*

Of course, this recipe was given by Apicius for a whole animal. To season a 2–3 lb. roast use the adapted quantities of ingredients, combine, and simmer for 20 minutes before serving with the meat.

## Lamb or Kid in Cream Sauce

*3–4 lb. lamb or kid roast*

Season meat with salt and pepper. Roast in a 325°F oven for 2 hours or until done.

*Sauce:*
*¼ t. ground pepper*
*½ t. thyme*
*½ t. celery seed (or lovage)*
*2 t. butter*
*1 T. flour*
*⅔ c. white wine*
*⅔ c. cream*
*1 T. roasting pan liquid*

For the sauce, grind together pepper, thyme, celery seed (or lovage). In a saucepan, melt butter and stir in flour to make a paste. Mix with wine, spices, and bring to a boil. Simmer and carefully stir in cream and liquid from roasting pan. Serve with slices of roast meat.

## Marinated Lamb or Kid in Savory Sauce

*3–4 lb. lamb or kid roast*

*Marinade:*
*2 t. ground pepper*
*1 t. rosemary (or rue)*
*1½ t. savory*
*2 onions, finely chopped*
*1 t. thyme*
*2 c. vegetable or beef stock*

*Sauce:*
*1 t. savory*
*pinch of rosemary (or rue)*
*1 onion, finely chopped*
*¼ c. dates, finely chopped*
*1 c. meat stock or pan juices*
*¼ c. red wine*
*¼ c. boiled red wine*
*2 t. olive oil*

Marinate the roast (or whole prepared animal) half a day in a covered pan containing the pepper, rosemary (or rue), savory, chopped onion, thyme, and stock. Baste occasionally.

Roast in a fresh pan in a 325°F oven with a little olive oil.

Meanwhile, prepare the sauce. Grind savory and rosemary (or rue) together. Add to chopped onion and dates. Blend with the stock, red wine, boiled wine (see p. 3) and 2 t. olive oil. Twenty minutes before serving, when roast is nearly done, pour the sauce over it and cook together, letting the sauce thicken.

*Serve the meat in the sauce, along with new sweet peas and roast potatoes. The flavors of rosemary and savory highlight this exciting sauce.*

## Plum Sauce for Roast Lamb or Kid

*3–4 lb. lamb or kid roast*

*Sauce:*
*½ t. ground pepper*
*pinch of rosemary (or rue)*
*1 onion, finely chopped*
*¼ t. savory*
*6 damsons or plums, pitted*
*½ t. ginger*
*½ c. red wine*
*1 c. vegetable or beef stock*
*1 T. olive oil*
*mild wine or cider vinegar*

First roast the lamb or kid in a 325°F oven for 2 hours or until done.

Meanwhile, make a sauce with the following ingredients. Combine pepper, rosemary (or rue), chopped onion, savory, damsons or plums, ginger, red wine, stock, and olive oil. Bring the sauce to a boil, and simmer for 25 minutes to reduce. Pour over each serving at the table, and sprinkle with a little vinegar.

## Stuffed Roast Suckling Kid with Wine Sauce

*8–10 lb. suckling kid*

Roast the kid in a 325°F oven for 2 hours.

*Stuffing:*
*½ t. ground pepper*
*½ t. celery seed (or lovage)*
*½ t. ginger*
*2 cloves or 1 laurel berry*
*pinch of chamomile*
*1 lb. cooked, browned calf's brains*
*2 c. bread crumbs*
*1 raw egg*
*2 t. honey*
*7–8 sausage casings*
*grease-proof paper or foil*

To make the stuffing, first grind together pepper, celery seed (or lovage), ginger, and cloves (or laurel berry). Add chamomile. Chop cooked calf's brains, combine the bread crumbs, and well beaten egg sweetened with honey, and combine with seasonings to make forcemeats. Fill casings with this stuffing and tie into a ring.

Next, season the roast with the sauce made from stock, butter, and wine. Place the sausage on top, and return to the oven. After 1 hour remove the sausage, and, if it is a larger animal, continue roasting the kid 1 hour more.

*Sauce:*
*½ c. vegetable or chicken stock*
*1 T. butter*
*½ c. red wine*

Make the gravy by combining pan juices with pepper, celery seed (or lovage), and wine. Heat to a boil and add flour to thicken. Decorate the finished roast with the sausage ring, and serve slices of meat in the gravy.

For a more authentic version of the recipe, decorate the kid with a plaited crown of laurel before serving.

*Gravy:*
*pan juices*
*¼ t. ground pepper*
*½ t. celery seed (or lovage)*
*¼ c. red boiled wine (see p. 3)*
*pan juices*
*flour*
*laurel fronds*

*We traditionally cook this tremendous dish for Christmas dinner. Since the animals are generally born in the spring, our whole herd is frozen and kept for us at the butcher. A 10 pound roast stuffed suckling kid will satisfy a party of 12–14. Sweet potatoes and unseasoned carrots make good accompaniments.*

## Pork Roast Stuffed with Nuts and Sausage

*1 leg of pork*

*Stuffing:*
*½ t. ground pepper*
*1 t. celery seed (or lovage)*
*½ t. oregano*
*½ t. ginger*
*2 T. pork or chicken stock*
*1 lb. cooked calf's brains*
*1 raw egg*
*2 c. bread crumbs*
*⅓ c. cooked chicken breast, finely chopped*
*2 T. pine nuts or almonds, finely chopped*
*Pepper Sausage (see p. 10)*
*foil*

For the stuffing, in a mortar, grind together pepper, celery seed (or lovage), oregano and ginger. Moisten with stock. Add to finely chopped calf's brains, and combine with bread crumbs, well beaten egg, chicken breast, and chopped nuts.

Bone the pork leg and fill with the stuffing. Cover the openings with foil and fasten with string. Roast in a 350°F oven, 35–40 minutes a pound.

Serve the roast pork leg with slices of Pepper (Myrtle) Sausage.

*The Romans loved pork. Most of Apicius' recipes are for whole suckling pigs, but I have altered amounts to suit the size of the roasts commonly available in North America. I like to serve Roman style pork with hot vegetables in season, and roast or boiled potatoes.*

## Roast Pork Apicius

*3–5 lb. pork roast*
*5 medium onions*
*3 t. cumin*
*1 t. ground ginger*
*1 t. thyme*
*1 t. coriander*
*1 c. pork or chicken stock*
*1 T. flour*
*ground pepper*

Liberally sprinkle the pork with cumin, and roast in a 350°F oven, 35 minutes per pound. After 1 hour, add ginger, thyme, and coriander. Add whole medium onions to the pan.

When the meat is done, use onions and drippings to make a gravy. Thicken the gravy with flour and serve with slices of pork sprinkled with pepper.

Since suckling pig is often difficult to obtain, some of these recipes substitute roast leg of pork or roast pork loin.

*Apicius shows us the versatility of cumin, which need not be limited to a supporting role in curry powders. It is particularly good here, where it is cooked into the meat during the first hour before the other spices.*

## Leg of Pork Stuffed with Sausage

6 lb. leg of pork

Stuffing:
½ t. ground pepper
1 t. celery seed (or lovage)
1 t. oregano
2 T. pork or chicken stock
1 lb. chopped, browned calf's brains
2 raw eggs
2 c. bread crumbs
½ lb. pork sausage, cooked, or Pepper Sausage (see p. 10)

In a mortar, grind together pepper, celery seed (or lovage), and oregano. Moisten with stock, and mix with chopped brains and bread crumbs. Bind with well beaten eggs, and combine with thinly sliced pieces of cooked pork or Pepper Sausage.

Debone the pork, fill the opening with the mixture, and cover with foil or tie with string. Roast in a 350°F oven for 3 to 3½ hours or till done. Serve the stuffing with a sprinkling of pepper.

*For convenience you can substitute extra pork sausage for the calf's brains. I particularly enjoy the flavors of celery seed, lovage, and oregano, and often double the quantities given here. Serve with* Turnips in Cumin Sauce, *and roast potatoes.*

## Roast Pork Stuffed with Bread and Honey

3–5 lb. roast of pork
Stuffing:
½ t. pepper
2 T. honey
½ c. red wine
1 bay leaf
2 c. bread crumbs

Debone the pork roast.

In a saucepan, mix pepper, honey, red wine, and bay leaf. Bring to a boil, stirring occasionally. Remove the bay leaf, and add bread crumbs. Simmer gently until the stuffing is smooth. (Add more wine if required.) Fill the pork roast. Bind the openings with string and wrap the stuffed roast in foil. Roast in a 350°F oven, 35 minutes per pound.

*In the original recipe Apicius did not include any meats in his stuffing. I like to add more body by using a mixture of pork sausage meat and liver, a spoonful of celery seed, and a little cumin. Serve with apple sauce, pan gravy, and steamed turnips and carrots, chopped up together.*

## Apicius' Cold Sauce for Roast Pork or Baked Ham

*Sauce:*
*¼ t. ground pepper*
*½ t. celery seed (or lovage)*
*½ t. coriander*
*pinch of mint*
*pinch of rosemary (or rue)*
*¾ c. pork or chicken stock*
*1 T. honey*
*¼ c. red wine*

Dry the cooked meat and serve with the following chilled sauce.

To make the sauce, in a mortar, grind together pepper, celery seed (or lovage), coriander, mint, and rosemary (or rue). Combine with stock, honey, and wine. Bring to a boil, then simmer slowly for 25 minutes to reduce. Chill, and serve with slices of meat.

## Vitellian Roast Pork with Onions

*3–5 lb. choice pork roast*

*Seasoning:*
*3 t. cumin*

Prepare the pork in the manner of wild boar by wiping the meat, then sprinkling it with cumin several hours before cooking. (See p. 128.)

Roast with onions, uncovered, in a 350°F oven, 35 minutes per pound.

*Sauce:*
*¼ t. ground pepper*
*1 t. celery seed (or lovage)*
*¾ c. stock*
*¼ c. red wine*
*1 T. butter or olive oil*
*4 onions*
*1 T. flour*

For the sauce, in a mortar, grind together pepper and celery seed (or lovage). Combine with stock, wine, and butter or olive oil. When the meat is done, take it out of the oven, set aside, preserving the pan juices and onions. Now, to the roasting pan add the sauce and simmer for 20 minutes, stirring occasionally. Thicken with flour, and serve with slices of meat.

*Despite being named after the cruel emperor Vitellius, this wine sauce is delicious.*

### Roast Pork in Celery Seed Sauce

*3–5 lb. choice pork roast*

*Seasoning:*
*2–3 t. cumin*

Prepare the roast pork in the manner of wild boar by first wiping the meat, then sprinkling it with cumin several hours before cooking. (See p. 128.) Roast uncovered in a 350°F oven, 35 minutes per pound.

*Sauce:*
*¼ t. ground pepper*
*1 t. celery seed (or lovage)*
*pinch each of caraway and fennel*
*1 t. rosemary (or rue)*
*1 c. pork or chicken stock*
*¼ c. red wine*
*1 T. butter or olive oil*
*flour*
*1 t. celery seed, ground*

For the sauce, grind together pepper, celery seed (or lovage), caraway, fennel, and rosemary (or rue). Blend with stock, red wine, and butter or olive oil. Put the sauce in a pan, bring to a boil, then simmer slowly for 25 minutes. Thicken with flour.

Remove the finished roast from the oven and sprinkle it with celery seed. Serve slices of meat with the sauce.

### Frontinian Pork with Anise and Chives

*3–5 lb. choice pork roast*

*Marinade:*
*½ c. red wine*
*1 c. pork or chicken stock*
*½ t. ground pepper*
*2 T. celery seed (or lovage)*
*1 t. coriander*

Marinate the pork roast in the wine marinade ingredients for about 4 hours, turning the meat from time to time. Then roast in a 350°F oven for 35 minutes per pound.

*Sauce:*
*1 c. pork or chicken stock*
*¼ c. red wine*
*2 T. chopped chives*
*pinch of aniseed*
*flour*

Remove roast from pan when done, and reserve pan juices. To these add the stock, chives, and aniseed, and simmer for 20 minutes. Then thicken with flour and serve with slices of meat. If you wish, sprinkle with pepper.

*Repeat the theme of the sauce by serving with baked potatoes with sour cream and chives, and, for color and taste, a dish of* Carrots Cooked with Cumin.

## *Roast Pork Crowned with Laurel*

*3–5 lb. choice pork roast*

Marinate the pork roast in the wine marinade ingredients for about 4 hours, turning the meat from time to time. Then roast in a 350°F oven for 35 minutes per pound.

*Marinade:*
*½ c. red wine*
*1 c. pork or chicken stock*
*½ t. ground pepper*
*2 t. celery seed (or lovage)*
*1 t. coriander*

*Sauce:*
*¼ t. ground pepper*
*1 t. celery seed (or lovage)*
*pinch of caraway*
*pinch of fennel*
*4 juniper berries or 2 cloves,*
*crushed*
*¾ c. pork or chicken stock*
*¼ c. red wine*
*1 T. butter or olive oil*
*flour*
*laurel fronds*

For the sauce, in a mortar, grind pepper, celery seed (or lovage), caraway, fennel, and juniper berries or cloves. Blend with stock, wine, and olive oil or butter. Bring to a boil, simmer slowly for 25 minutes, then thicken with flour. Plait laurel leaves into a crown and decorate the roast.

At the table, drench slices of pork with the sauce, and serve.

*In the Pacific Northwest, the dramatic visual effect of a plaited laurel crown can be imitated with salal.*

## Marinated Pork Cooked in Two Wine Sauces

*3–5 lb. choice pork roast*

*Marinade:*
*½ c. red wine*
*1 c. pork or chicken stock*
*½ t. ground pepper*
*2 T. celery seed (or lovage)*
*2 t. coriander*

Marinate the pork roast in the wine marinade ingredients for about 4 hours, turning from time to time. Then roast in a 350°F oven for 35 minutes per pound.

When the roast has been half cooked, add the first sauce, basting the meat with it.

*First sauce:*
*2 T. olive oil or butter*
*¼ c. stock*
*¼ c. red wine*
*¼ c. water*
*1 T. chopped chives*
*1 t. coriander*
*¼ c. red wine*

For this sauce, combine olive oil or butter, stock, red wine, water, chopped chives, and coriander, and add to the roast. After 1 hour, add more red wine.

*Second sauce:*
*½ t. ground pepper*
*½ t. lovage (or celery seed)*
*pinch of caraway*
*½ t. celery seed*
*½ t. ginger*
*½ c. pork or chicken stock*
*¼ c. gravy from roasting pan*
*¼ c. sweet raisin wine or muscatel*
*flour*
*ground pepper*

For the second sauce, grind together pepper, lovage (or celery seed), caraway, celery seed, and ginger. Combine with stock, gravy from the roast, and sweet wine. Bring this sauce to a boil, simmer slowly for 25 minutes to reduce, or thicken with flour. Place the meat on a serving platter and drench it with this sauce. Sprinkle with pepper and serve.

*So much careful seasoning is lavished upon this superb roast that the accompaniments should be very simple. I like plain boiled new potatoes garnished with a little butter and sprigs of parsley, and lightly steamed broccoli.*

## Roast Suckling Pig with Garden Vegetables

*10–12 lb. suckling pig*

Dress the pig by removing organs and cleaning the interior.

*Stuffing:*
*1 c. cooked chicken meat, finely chopped*
*1 c. thinly sliced cooked pork sausage*
*½ c. pitted dates*
*1 large onion, finely chopped*
*1 c. chopped beets*
*2 c. chopped celery*
*1 small cabbage chopped*
*½ c. blanched almonds, whole*
*2 t. ground pepper*
*4–5 c. bread crumbs*
*3–4 raw eggs*
*(pork or chicken stock)*

For the stuffing, combine chicken, sausage, chopped dates, chopped onion, beets, celery, cabbage, almonds, pepper, and bread crumbs. Add well beaten eggs to bind, and stock to moisten, if necessary. Stuff the pig. (If necessary increase the stuffing to suit the size of the animal.) Finish by securing the ear flaps with skewers.

Roast in a 350°F oven for 35 minutes per pound. An hour before it is done, put an apple in the pig's mouth.

*Sauce:*
*¼ t. ground pepper*
*½ t. rosemary*
*1 c. pork or chicken stock*
*½ c. red wine*
*1 t. honey*
*2 T. butter*
*flour*

For the sauce, grind together pepper and rosemary. Combine with stock, wine, honey, and butter. Heat the sauce and baste the pig frequently with the liquid. When the meat is cooked, simmer the pan drippings combined with the sauce, and thicken with flour. Serve with the roast pig as a gravy.

*The richness and complexity of the stuffing really precludes the need for any side dishes, except perhaps, crisply roasted potatoes.*

## Cold Condiment for Ham

*1 medium cooked ham*

Use a ham that is not heavily salted.

*Sauce:*
*½ t. ground pepper*
*pinch each of caraway and aniseed*
*½ t. oregano*
*2 T. pine nuts or almonds, finely chopped*
*1 T. cider vinegar*
*dash of fish-pickle (see p. 2)*
*1 t. anchovy paste*
*2 dates, finely chopped*
*1 t. honey*
*½ t. ground mustard*
*4 T. olive oil*
*ground pepper*

In a mortar, grind together pepper, caraway, aniseed, and oregano. To this add chopped nuts, then moisten with vinegar and a little fish-pickle. Add chopped dates, honey, and mustard. Blend with olive oil, and add a sprinkling of pepper. Serve cold with cold ham slices.

*This is very good eaten outdoors with hard-boiled farm eggs, and slices of bread and butter, and washed down with a glass of very cold sparkling cider. (The Romans ate picnic lunches, too.)*

## Marinated Pork Chops

*2 lbs. ¾" pork chops*

*Marinade:*
*½ c. red wine*
*½ c. chicken stock*
*2 t. cider vinegar*
*½ t. ground pepper*
*½ t. cumin*

Marinate chops for 4 hours in wine marinade ingredients, turning from time to time. Then sauté in butter or olive oil till done.

*These pork chops are simple but very agreeable. Serve with* Beans (or peas) in the Pod in Coriander Sauce, *and a dish of sautéed apple rounds, or plain apple sauce.*

## *Rabbit or Hare in Onion Fennel Sauce*

*3 lb rabbit, or hare*

*Sauce:*
*olive oil or butter*
*½ t. ground pepper*
*½ t. lovage (or celery seed)*
*¼ t. savory*
*1 small onion, chopped*
*pinch of rosemary (or rue)*
*½ t. celery seed*
*1 c. chicken stock*
*¼ t. fennel*
*½ c. white wine*
*1 T. olive oil*

Put the rabbit into a covered pan and braise gently for ½ hour. Remove, wipe, and brush with oil or butter. Cook covered, in a 350°F oven in a stewing pot for 30 minutes. Then brush a second time with oil or butter, and cook a further 30 minutes. Lastly, uncover the pot and cook the rabbit for 30 minutes in the following sauce.

In a mortar, grind together pepper, lovage (or celery seed), savory, chopped onion, rosemary (or rue), and celery seed. Combine with stock, fennel, wine, and olive oil. Add this sauce to the rabbit, and cook 30 minutes, basting from time to time. Serve the rabbit in its own gravy.

*Rabbit meat is rich and easily accepts the flavors of such herbs as celery, lovage, rosemary, and savory. Sip a deep glass of Burgundy with these rabbit dishes, to evoke the flavor of ancient Roman wines.*

## Braised Rabbit or Hare in a Sweet Wine Sauce

*3 lb. rabbit, or hare*
*½ t. ground pepper*
*¼ c. dates, finely chopped*
*pinch of fennel*
*⅛ c. raisins*
*¼ c. boiled sweet wine (see p. 3)*
*1 c. chicken stock*
*1 T. olive oil*
*ground pepper*

Prepare and cook the rabbit according to the preceding recipe, but cook in the following sauce for the last 30 minutes. Combine pepper, chopped dates, fennel, raisins, wine, stock, and olive oil. Braise the rabbit in this sauce, basting from time to time. Serve with a sprinkling of pepper.

## Stuffed Rabbit or Hare

*3 lb. rabbit or hare*
*Stuffing:*
*¼ c. chopped almonds or walnuts*
*¼ t. ground pepper*
*¾ c. pork sausage meat*
*1 raw egg*
*1 c. bread crumbs*
*Sauce:*
*pinch of rosemary (or rue)*
*½ t. ground pepper*
*1 small onion, finely chopped*
*½ t. savory*
*¼ c. dates, chopped*
*¾ c. chicken stock*
*¼ c. boiled red wine (see p. 3) or Spiced Wine Apicius (see p. 4)*

Roast the stuffed rabbit in a 325°F oven in a covered pan for 1½ hours. Then uncover and finish cooking in the sauce.

To make the stuffing mix nuts with pepper, sausage meat, bread crumbs, well beaten egg to bind, and a little of the pan juices. Stuff the rabbit and tie with string or secure with skewers. Roast until done.

To make the sauce, grind together rosemary (or rue), pepper, and savory. Mix with chopped onion and dates, then combine with stock and wine.

Then, when rabbit has baked for 1½ hours, uncover it and finish it in this sauce for 30 minutes more, basting from time to time. Serve meat with the sauce thickened with flour.

*This recipe is among my favorites, and does very well at dinner parties. Two stuffed, three pound animals will serve eight. Precede with* Watercress Salad *and a glass of* Spiced Wine Apicius.

## Roast Rabbit or Hare in Thick Cumin Sauce

*3 lb. rabbit or hare*

*Sauce:*
*¼ t. ground pepper*
*½ t. celery seed (or lovage)*
*¾ t. cumin*
*1 hard-boiled egg yolk*
*1 c. chicken stock*
*½ c. white wine*
*1 T. olive oil*
*1 t. wine vinegar or cider vinegar*
*¼ c. shallots or onion, chopped*
*1 t. oregano or 1 t. savory*

Roast the rabbit in a 325°F oven in a covered pan for 1½ hours. Uncover, add the following sauce, and cook for about 30 minutes more, basting occasionally.

For the sauce, in a mortar, grind pepper, celery seed (or lovage), cumin, and the hard-boiled yolk. Mix well and form into a ball. In a saucepan, simmer stock, white wine, olive oil, vinegar, and shallots or onion. Add the ball of seasonings and stir in oregano or savory. Simmer to reduce for 15–30 minutes, and serve over the roast meat.

## Rabbit Stuffed with Liver and Sausage

*3 lb. rabbit*
*¼ t. ground pepper*
*1 t. oregano*
*½ t. cumin*
*¼ lb. rabbit liver, chopped*
*½ c. ground pork sausage meat*
*1 small onion, chopped*
*½ c. bread crumbs*
*1 raw egg yolk*
*1 t. cumin (for the skin of the rabbit)*
*3 T. butter*

Clean the inside of the rabbit, and reserve the liver. To make the stuffing, grind together pepper, oregano, and cumin. Add to chopped liver, sausage meat, onion, and bread crumbs. Bind with well beaten egg yolk. Now, stuff the animal, and secure opening with string. Moisten the skin of the rabbit with butter and season with cumin.

Place in a greased roasting pan, and cook in a 300°F oven for 1½ hours, basting from time to time.

*Very good served with new potatoes and gravy made from the pan juices. Though the Romans did not have potatoes, Apicius would have approved of this combination. The stuffing must be made with pure sausage meats. Otherwise the delicate balance of seasonings will be upset.*

## Rabbit or Hare Served in Its Own Gravy

*3 lb. rabbit or hare*

*Seasoning:*
*1 T. olive oil*
*1 c. chicken stock*
*¼ c. reduced chicken stock*
*2 t. chives*
*1 t. coriander*
*pinch of aniseed*

In a stewing pot, put olive oil, stock, chives, coriander, and aniseed. Cut up rabbit into pieces and add to pot. Cover, bring to a boil, and cook rabbit for 1 hour over low heat.

*Sauce:*
*¼ t. ground pepper*
*1 t. celery seed (or lovage)*
*½ t. cumin*
*½ t. coriander*
*pinch of fennel*
*1 t. mint*
*pinch of rosemary (or rue)*
*1 small onion, chopped*
*2 t. honey*
*½ c. stewing pan juices*
*½ c. boiled red wine (see p. 3)*
*1 t. white wine or cider vinegar*
*flour*
*pepper*

For the sauce, in a mortar grind pepper, celery seed (or lovage), cumin, coriander seeds, fennel, mint, and a pinch of rosemary (or rue). Add onion, and combine with honey, liquid from the rabbit pan, boiled wine, and vinegar.

Uncover the rabbit, add the sauce to the stewing pan, and cook for a further 30 minutes. Thicken sauce with flour, and serve the meat drenched in sauce. Sprinkle with pepper at the table.

*I am surprised that people do not eat more rabbit. The meat is relatively inexpensive and readily absorbs seasonings. In my experience they benefit from long, slow cooking. This also allows you to grind herbs for the sauce, and prepare the vegetables.*

## *Rabbit or Hare with Wine Sauce*

*3 lb. rabbit or hare*

*Sauce:*
*½ t. ground pepper*
*1 t. celery seed (or lovage)*
*¾ c. chicken stock*
*¼ c. white wine*
*roasting pan juices*
*1 T. olive oil, or butter*
*flour*
*ground pepper*

Roast the rabbit in a 325°F oven for 1½ hours or until tender, basting frequently with wine sauce to moisten the skin. To make the sauce, in a mortar, grind pepper and celery seed (or lovage). Add these to stock, wine, pan juices, and olive oil or butter. Heat and baste rabbit with the sauce. Before serving, thicken sauce with flour, then pour over the meat with a sprinkling of pepper.

## *Stuffed Rabbit or Hare with Wine Sauce*

*3 lb. rabbit or hare*

*Stuffing:*
*¾ c. pork sausage meat*
*¼ c. chopped almonds*
*1 c. bread crumbs*
*1 raw egg*
*chicken stock*

*1 ½ c. wine sauce (see p. 3)*

For the stuffing, combine pork sausage, meat, almonds, bread crumbs, and well beaten egg. Add a touch of chicken stock, and stuff the rabbit. Secure opening with string or skewers, and roast in a 325°F oven for 1½ hours. Baste frequently with wine sauce, and serve the roast with 1 cup of the heated wine sauce at the table.

*This is a very easy recipe, and yet the flavor is unmistakably Roman. I prefer to chop the almonds only in half. You can add a little pepper and cumin as well, if you wish. Delicious served with Steamed Squash Sautéed with Cumin, and a dish of saffron rice.*

## Richly Stuffed Rabbit or Hare with Wine Sauce

*3 lb. rabbit or hare*

*Stuffing:*
*½ t. ground pepper*
*1 t. celery seed (or lovage)*
*1 t. oregano*
*2 T. chicken stock*
*½ c. cooked chicken livers, chopped*
*¼ c. cooked calf's brains, chopped*
*½ c. cooked chicken, chopped*
*1 raw egg*

*butter*

*Sauce:*
*¼ t. ground pepper*
*1 t. celery seed (or lovage)*
*1 c. chicken stock*
*½ c. white wine*
*¼ c. pan juices*
*flour*
*ground pepper*

For the stuffing, in a mortar, grind together pepper, celery seed (or lovage), and oregano. Add stock. Mix. Now add chicken livers, calf's brains, and chicken. Mix with well beaten egg. Stuff the rabbit with this mixture, and secure opening with string or skewers. Roast in a 325°F oven for 1½ hours, basting frequently with wine sauce or butter.

For the sauce, combine pepper, celery seed (or lovage), stock, and wine. Add juices from the roasting pan. Bring the sauce to a boil, simmer for 25 minutes, and thicken with flour. Serve sauce at the table with the roast, and sprinkle with pepper.

*Calf's brains can be difficult to obtain, so I sometimes use pork sausage meat instead. Lovage is preferable to celery seeds, but this most popular green herb of the ancient world is little known today. It grows profusely in our herb garden. Write to me in care of the publisher, and I will send you some seeds.*

## Thyme Sauce for Braised Rabbit or Hare

*3 lb. braised rabbit or hare*

*Sauce:*
*3–4 medium onions, sliced*
*2 T. olive oil*
*¾ c. chicken stock*
*1 t. white wine vinegar or cider vinegar*
*¼ c. white wine*
*¼ t. rosemary (or rue)*
*1 t. ground thyme*
*flour*

Sauté onion in olive oil. Add stock, vinegar, wine, rosemary (or rue), and thyme. Simmer for 10–15 minutes, then thicken with flour, and pour over the cooked rabbit. Serve.

*Serve with fried parsnips and boiled new potatoes.*

## Seasoned Liver Sauce for Rabbit or Hare

*3 lb. braised rabbit or hare*

*Sauce:*
*½ t. ground pepper*
*pinch of rosemary (or rue)*
*1 c. chicken stock*
*¼ c. shallots or onion*
*¼ c. cooked chicken livers,*
*chopped*
*½ c. white wine*
*1 T. olive oil or butter*

In a mortar, grind together pepper and rosemary (or rue). Add stock, chopped shallots or onion, the chopped liver, wine, and olive oil. Bring to a boil, then reduce for 25 minutes, and serve over rabbit.

*If you keep your own rabbits or know someone who does, use the liver of the animal. In this case also increase the quantity of rosemary to one teaspoon, crushed, or a small "branch," whole, in the sauce.*

## Marinated and Basted Rabbit or Hare

*3 lb. rabbit or hare*
*Marinade:*
*2 t. peppercorns*
*½ t. rosemary (or rue)*
*1 t. savory*
*2 onions, chopped*
*1 t. thyme*
*2 c. chicken stock*

*Sauce:*
*½ t. ground pepper*
*pinch of rosemary (or rue)*
*½ t. savory*
*3 small whole onions*
*¼ c. dates, chopped, or raisins*
*½ c. white wine*
*1 T. olive oil or butter*
*2 c. chicken stock*
*(flour)*
*ground pepper*

Marinate rabbit pieces 8 hours in a covered dish with pepper, rosemary (or rue), savory, onions, thyme, and stock. Baste occasionally.

Combine pepper, rosemary (or rue), savory, onions, dates or raisins, wine, olive oil or butter, and stock in a stewing pan. To this sauce, add the marinated meat, and cook on the stove for 1 hour, or until tender, stirring from time to time to distribute the seasonings. When done, thicken the sauce with flour, if you wish. Serve with the meat, and add a sprinkling of pepper.

*People need not worry about using rue. It thrives in my herb garden, and in spite of Shakespeare, it is in fact deliciously bitter—the innocent victim of "bad press."*

## Well Seasoned Rabbit or Hare

*3 lb. rabbit or hare*

*Seasoning:*
*½ c. boiled white wine (see*
*p. 3) or must*
*½ c. chicken stock*
*1 t. ground mustard seed*
*pinch of aniseed*
*2 whole leeks*
*½ c. water*

Braise the rabbit in a 325°F oven for 1½ hours in the following seasonings.

For the seasonings, combine wine, stock, mustard, aniseed, and leeks. Stir occasionally and make sure the leeks remain covered with liquid.

*Sauce:*
*½ t. ground pepper*
*½ t. savory*
*one onion ring*
*4 dates, chopped*
*4 plums (or damsons), sliced*
*¼ c. white wine*
*½ c. chicken stock*
*¼ c. boiled wine (see p. 3)*
*1 T. olive oil or butter*
*(flour)*
*(pepper)*

For the sauce, grind together pepper and savory, and add these to onion, dates, plums (or damsons), wine, stock, and olive oil or butter. Bring the mixture to a boil, then simmer slowly for 25 minutes. Thicken with flour, if you wish. Serve the sauce with the rabbit and leeks. Sprinkle with pepper if you wish.

# The Sea

# Book Nine

## OF LOBSTERS

*In winter lobsters seek out sunny coasts, but in summer they withdraw into the shade of the sea. All members of this [bloodless] class are afflicted by winter but become fat in the autumn and spring, and even more so at the full moon since by night the moon makes them mellow by the warmth of its gleams.*

Pliny.

IUS IN LOCUSTA ET CAMMARI  *Sauce for Lobster and Crayfish*  Brown chopped pallacanian onions...Add pepper, lovage, caraway, cumin, a date, honey, vinegar, wine, fish stock, oil, and boiled new wine. Add mustard to the sauce while it is still boiling.

LOCUSTAS ASSAS SIC FACIES  *Roast Lobsters*  Open the lobsters, as is customary, and then leave them in their shells. Pour pepper sauce and coriander sauce over them, [cover] and roast on a gridiron. When they become dry, pour more sauce over the gridiron. Repeat this as often as necessary until they are roasted well and then serve.

LOCUSTA ELIXA CUM CUMINATO  *Boiled Lobster with Cumin Sauce*  Pepper, lovage, parsley, dried mint, more of cumin, honey, vinegar, and fish stock. If you like, add spikenard and cinnamon.

ALITER LOCUSTA  *Lobster*  Make lobster-tail forcemeats this way. Remove the harmful flesh. Boil [thoroughly] and chop into small pieces. Then shape into forcemeats with stock and pepper, and eggs.

IN LOCUSTA ELIXA  *[Sauce] for Boiled Lobster*  Pepper, cumin, rue, honey, vinegar, fish stock, and olive oil.

ALITER IN LOCUSTA  *[Sauce] for Lobster*  Pepper, lovage, cumin, mint, rue, nuts, honey, vinegar, fish stock, and wine.

## OF RAY

IN TORPEDINE  *Of Ray*  Grind pepper, rue, and a small dried onion. Add honey, fish stock, some raisin wine, a little wine, and drops of good quality olive oil. Taste, and add a little olive oil if necessary. When [the sauce] has begun to boil, thicken with starch. [Pour over the cooked ray and serve.]

## Spiced Sauce for Lobster or Crab

*2½ lbs. lobster or crab meat*
*2 T. chopped onion or shallots*
*2 t. olive oil or butter*
*¼ t. ground pepper*
*1 t. celery seed (or lovage)*
*pinch of caraway*
*¼ t. cumin*
*¼ c. dates, chopped*
*1 t. honey*
*1 t. white wine vinegar or cider vinegar*
*½ c. white wine*
*⅔ c. shellfish stock*
*2 t. olive oil*
*⅓ c. boiled white wine*
*pinch of mustard seed*

First brown onion or shallots in olive oil or butter. Grind together pepper, celery seed (or lovage), caraway, cumin, and dates. Add to the cooked shallots or onion. Blend with honey, vinegar, wine, fish stock, olive oil, and boiled wine. Bring to a boil, and add mustard. Reduce for 25–30 minutes, and serve hot over the lobster or crabmeat.

*For a classical lunch for two, you can strain the sauce and season half a cup of cooked lobster or crab meats with it. Fold this into a plain omelette, and garnish it with parsley sprigs. Delicious with a glass of chilled, dry white wine.*

## Lobster Baked in Two Sauces

*2½–3 lb. lobster*
*Pepper sauce:*
*1 T. mild fish-pickle to each generous dash pepper*
*Coriander sauce:*
*1 t. coriander*
*pinch of aniseed*
*½ t. oregano*
*¼ t. ground pepper*
*1 t. honey*
*¼ c. white wine*
*¾ c. lobster stock*
*2 t. olive oil*
*1 t. white or cider vinegar*

Plunge the lobster in boiling water for 3 minutes, then split the lobster in two along its length. Season, to taste, with the pepper sauce, and then the coriander sauce below, and bake.

For the coriander sauce, grind together coriander, aniseed, oregano, and pepper. Combine with honey, wine, fish stock, olive oil, and vinegar. Heat to a boil, then simmer slowly for 5 minutes.

After seasoning the lobster with this sauce, bake for 25–30 minutes in a 325°F oven or over coals, basting with olive oil or butter. Add more olive oil as required to avoid drying out the flesh of the lobster. Serve.

## Boiled Lobster or Crab with Thick Cumin Sauce

*one 2½–3 lb. lobster, or 7–8 small crabs*

Boil the lobster or crabs for 25 minutes and reserve stock.

*Sauce:*
*¼ t. ground pepper*
*1 t. celery seed (or lovage)*
*1 t. parsley*
*1 t. mint*
*1 t. honey*
*¼ t. cumin*
*1 t. white or cider vinegar*
*1 c. fish stock*
*1 bay or spikenard leaf*
*(dash of cinnamon)*

For the sauce, grind together pepper, celery seed (or lovage), parsley, mint, and cumin. Add honey, vinegar, and fish stock (to cover). Add bay leaf (or spikenard), and heat to a boil, then simmer to reduce the sauce for 25 minutes. Strain out bay leaf, and serve sauce as seasoning for the shelled lobster or crab pieces.

If you like, add a dash of cinnamon in the last five minutes to the simmering sauce.

*As everyone's taste is unique, you may wish to add more cumin, if it is one of your favorites.*

## Simple Sauce for Boiled Lobsters or Crabs

*2½–3 lb. lobster, or 7–8 small crabs*

Boil lobster or crabs for 25 minutes and reserve stock.

*Sauce:*
*½ t. cumin*
*pinch of rosemary (or rue)*
*1 t. honey*
*3 t. olive oil or butter*
*½ c. lobster stock*

Combine cumin with rosemary (or rue), honey, olive oil or butter, and lobster stock. Bring to a boil, pour over lobster or crabs, and serve together. Or serve over the shelled meats.

*Apicius used rue, which in this instance is better than rosemary. Very good served as an hors d'oeuvre with sticks of toast, or crackers, or as a main course on a bed of rice.*

### Sauce for Boiled Lobster

*2½–3 lb. lobster*  Boil lobster for 25 minutes and reserve stock.

*Sauce:*
*½ t. ground pepper*
*1 t. celery seed (or lovage)*
*¼ t. cumin*
*1 t. mint or*
*pinch of rosemary (or rue)*
*¼ c. pine nuts or blanched*
*almonds, chopped*
*1 t. honey*
*2 t. white or cider vinegar*
*1 c. lobster stock*
*½ c. white wine*

In a mortar, grind together pepper, celery seed (or lovage), cumin, mint, and rosemary (or rue). Add to nuts, then blend with honey, vinegar, stock, and white wine. Bring to a boil, then simmer to reduce for 25 minutes. Serve with shelled lobster meat.

*Lobster can, of course, be delicious served simply with a little hot butter; but eaten this way lobster is quite wonderful. Add a lettuce and tomato salad and a very cold, very dry white wine.*

### Rosemary Sauce for Poached Skate

*½ lb. skate*

Poach the wings of the skate in water or fish stock till done.

*Sauce:*
*½ t. ground pepper*
*pinch of rosemary (or rue)*
*1 medium onion, finely chopped*
*1 t. honey*
*¾ c. fish stock*
*¼ c. white wine*
*olive oil*
*(flour)*

To make the sauce, grind together pepper and rosemary (or rue). Add to onion, and blend with honey, stock, wine, and olive oil to taste. Bring the sauce to a boil, then simmer for 25 minutes to reduce. (Or, if desired, thicken with flour.) Pour over each serving of the poached fish, and serve.

*Skate may be difficult to obtain, but this sauce and the one below are pleasant sauces for a variety of mild-flavored fishes.*

### Sharp Sauce for Poached Skate

*½ lb. skate*

Prepare fish as in previous recipe.

*Sauce:*
*½ t. ground pepper*
*1 t. celery seed (or lovage)*
*½ t. oregano*
*2 t. fresh parsley*
*3 fresh mint leaves*
*1 t. honey*
*1 c. fish stock*
*¼ c. white wine*
*2 T. olive oil or butter*
*(dash of mustard seed)*
*(1 t. white or cider vinegar)*
*(¼ c. raisins)*

In a mortar, grind together pepper, celery seed (or lovage), and oregano. Add chopped parsley and mint. Blend with honey, stock, white wine, and olive oil or butter. (If you like, add mustard and vinegar, and, for a livelier flavor, raisins.) Bring to a boil, then simmer to reduce for 25–30 minutes, and serve over each portion of the poached skate.

## Sautéed Squid in Wine Sauce

*1 lb. squid, fresh or canned*
*2 T. olive oil*
*½ t. ground pepper*
*¼ t. rosemary (or rue)*
*1 t. honey*
*1 c. fish stock*
*¼ c. white wine*
*(flour)*

Clean squid, cut up, and sauté the pieces in olive oil, then finish in the sauce for 40 minutes over low heat.

For the sauce, grind together pepper, rosemary (or rue). Add honey, stock, and wine. Bring to a boil, then pour over the pan of squid, and cook slowly together.

If desired, add flour at the end to make a thick sauce.

*Though not known to the Romans, two large sliced tomatoes make an excellent addition to the sauce. Canned squid may be used without alteration. (Dried squid must be well soaked before use, and even then is inferior to fresh or canned squid.)*

## Sausage Stuffed Squid

*2 lbs. squid*

*Stuffing:*
*2 T. olive oil*
*½ c. finely chopped pork sausage meat*
*½ t. ground pepper*
*1 t. lovage (or celery seed)*
*½ t. coriander*
*½ t. celery seed*
*1 egg yolk*

*Sauce:*
*1 t. honey*
*1 t. white or cider vinegar*
*1 c. fish stock*
*½ c. white wine*
*2 T. olive oil*

Clean the squid and cut off the tentacles.

To make the stuffing, cut up tentacles very finely and fry in olive oil. Mix together with sausage meat. Season with pepper, lovage (or celery seed), coriander, and celery seed. Bind with well beaten egg.

Fill each squid with stuffing and secure with toothpicks. Cook gently in the following wine sauce for 30 minutes.

For the sauce, combine honey, vinegar, stock, wine, and olive oil, cook squid with it, and serve together.

*I generally serve these squid dishes with steamed rice. Though squid are not pretty, they are very delicious when served Roman style.*

## Sauce for Stuffed Squid or Cuttlefish

*2 lbs. cooked stuffed squid (see*
*next recipe)*

*Sauce:*
*¼ t. ground pepper*
*½ t. lovage (or celery seed)*
*½ t. celery seed*
*pinch of caraway*
*1 t. honey*
*¾ c. beef stock*
*¼ c. white wine*

In a mortar, grind together pepper, lovage (or celery seed), celery seed, and caraway. Mix with honey, stock, and white wine. Bring to a boil, then simmer for 25 minutes to reduce. Pour over the sliced, stuffed squid, and serve.

This sauce may also be used with the *Sausage Stuffed Squid* above.

## Squid or Cuttlefish Stuffed with Brains

*2 lbs. squid*
*2 T. olive oil*
*¼ lb. calf's brains*
*butter*
*peppercorns*
*½ c. finely chopped*
*pork sausage*
*1 raw egg*
*½ t. ground pepper*
*pinch of fennel*

Clean squid, cut off tentacles, and chop them very finely. Fry the pieces in olive oil. Next, brown calf's brains in butter, and chop very finely. Mix tentacles and brains together with pork sausage. Bind with well beaten egg, and season with pepper. Stuff the squid and secure each with toothpicks. Cover with water seasoned with fennel, and cook 1 hour over low heat.

*If you prefer to omit the brains, or if they are un-available, use pepper sausage instead.*

*I'm just arrived from Baiae*
*An oyster drunk from Lake Lucrine:*
*But wanton though I am*
*I still can crave your noble sauce.*

Martial.

## Cumin-Cinnamon Sauce for Oysters

¼ t. pepper
1 t. celery seed (or lovage)
¼ t. cumin
2 t. parsley
½ t. mint
pinch of cinnamon
1 t. honey
1 t. white wine vinegar or cider vinegar
1 c. shellfish stock

In a mortar, grind pepper, celery seed (or lovage), parsley, mint, cumin, and cinnamon. Add to honey, vinegar, and shellfish stock. Bring to a boil, then gently simmer for 20 minutes to reduce.

*This is a sharp, pungent sauce to be used as a court bouillon in which to cook oysters and other shellfish. It is also very good, and worth trying without the cinnamon.*

## Fennel Sauce for Fish

⅛ t. fennel
¼ t. ground pepper
2 t. parsley
½ t. mint
1 t. honey
1 t. white wine vinegar or cider vinegar
1 c. fish stock

Combine fennel with pepper, parsley, mint, honey, vinegar, and stock. Bring to a boil, then gently simmer for 20 minutes to reduce.

*Fennel is a wonderfully refreshing flavor with fish.*

## *Thick Sauce for Squid or Cuttlefish*

2 lbs. cooked squid

*Sauce:*
½ t. ground pepper
½ t. celery seed (or lovage)
½ t. coriander
½ t. mint
1 raw egg yolk
1 t. honey
¾ c. fish stock
¼ c. white wine
1 t. white or cider vinegar
2 t. olive oil or butter

To make the sauce, grind together pepper, celery seed (or lovage), coriander, and mint. Mix with honey, stock, white wine, vinegar, and olive oil. Heat and carefully stir in well beaten egg yolk. Bring to a boil and simmer slowly to thicken. Serve with boiled or sautéed squid. If you wish, thicken the sauce further with flour before serving.

## *Seasoned Octopus*

2 lbs. octopus meat
3 T. fish-pickle (see p. 2)
½ t. ground pepper
¼ t. fennel

Clean octopus. Pound meat to tenderize, then cut body and tentacles into small pieces and cook till tender. Combine fish-pickle, pepper, and fennel, and season the cooked meat with the mixture before serving.

*Octopus is tough. To tenderize it, I thrash it on a rock.*

## *Oyster Stew with Wine*

3 c. shelled oysters
½ t. ground pepper
1 t. celery seed (or lovage)
1 t. white or cider vinegar
2 t. olive oil or butter
½ c. white wine
1½ c. oyster stock
2 raw egg yolks
1 T. flour
(honey)

Put oysters into a stewing pan, and season with pepper, celery seed (or lovage), vinegar, olive oil or butter, white wine, and strained oyster stock. Simmer for 20 minutes, stirring from time to time. At the end, beat the yolks, mix with flour, and add liquid from the oyster stew to make a smooth paste. Add to the stew, thicken, and serve.

If you wish, add a little honey to sweeten.

*Delicious served as a first course, or add chopped clams and tomatoes to create a chowder.*

# The Sea

## OF ALL KINDS OF SHELLFISH

IN OMNE GENUS CONCHYLIORUM *For All Kinds of Shellfish*
[Prepare them with] pepper, lovage, parsley, dried mint, a goodly
quantity of cumin, honey, stock and if you wish, add some cinnamon
and spikenard.

## OF SEA URCHINS

*Demetrius of Scepsis says that a Spartan once went to a feast and
sea urchins were placed on his table. He picked one up, not
understanding which part was edible, nor turning to his dinner
companions for advice. At once, he put it into his mouth intending
to tear it to pieces, shell and all. When he found the sea urchin
difficult to chew and couldn't understand the reason for its
sharpness, he declared, "Bloody food, I won't be weak now and give
it up but I'll never take another."*

Athenaeus.

IN ECHINO *Of Sea Urchin* Take a fresh saucepan [and pour
into it] a little olive oil, stock, sweet wine, and finely ground pepper.
Boil. Then add some [sauce] to each sea urchin. [Cook them over a
slow fire.] Stirring repeatedly, allow to boil three times. Sprinkle with
pepper and serve.

ALITER IN ECHINO *[Sauce] for Sea Urchin* Use pepper, a little
costmary, dried mint, honey wine, stock, and Indian spikenard and bay
leaf.

ALITER IN ECHINO *Sea Urchin* Put the sea urchins alone in
hot water only, cook, then lift them out and arrange them in a small
pan. Now add bayleaf, pepper, honey, stock, a little olive oil, and eggs
to thicken [the mixture]. Cook [the sea urchins and the sauce] in the
thermospodium. Sprinkle with pepper and serve.

*The hedgehog of the sea has a shell that's sharp
And only your bleeding fingers can touch the softness
that lie beneath*

Martial.

## Cumin Sauce for All Kinds of Shellfish

*½ t. ground pepper*
*¼ t. celery seed (or lovage)*
*½ t. fresh parsley*
*½ t. fresh mint*
*cumin, to taste*
*1 c. shellfish liquid*
*1 t. honey*
*1 t. white or cider vinegar*
*(pinch of bay leaf)*
*(dash of cinnamon)*
*(flour)*

In a mortar, grind together pepper, celery seed (or lovage), and cumin to taste. Add finely chopped parsley and mint. Mix with shellfish liquid, honey, and vinegar. (If you like, also add crushed bay leaf and cinnamon.) Bring to a boil, then simmer 25 minutes to reduce.

This sauce can be used as a court bouillon in the preparation of oysters, cockles, scallops, or mussels. For use with clams, thicken with flour, if you wish.

*The presence of cinnamon in a recipe for shellfish startled me at first. I should have known better than to doubt Apicius—it works wonderfully well here.*

## Sea Urchins Cooked in Wine Sauce

*20–30 sea urchins*
*Sauce:*
*2 t. olive oil*
*1 c. fish stock*
*2 T. sweet white wine*
*dash of ground pepper*

In a pan, combine olive oil, stock, and wine. Add a very small quantity of pepper. Bring this sauce to a boil, then simmer.

Meanwhile, remove the edible parts (the ovaries) of the sea urchins, and add them to the sauce. Simmer gently for 5 minutes. When cooked, remove from the sauce, sprinkle with pepper, and serve.

## Herb Sauce for Sea Urchins

*20–30 sea urchins*
*Sauce:*
*pinch each of costmary (or mint), pepper, and mint*
*2 T. sweet white wine (or mead)*
*1 c. fish stock*
*pinch of spikenard, or bay leaf, crushed*

Combine costmary (or mint), sweet wine (or mead), pepper, mint, fish stock, and spikenard or bay leaf. Heat the sauce, and cook the sea urchins as in the preceding recipe (*Sea Urchins Cooked in Wine Sauce*).

*Sea urchin ovaries are splendid by themselves, perhaps with a squeeze of lemon. They need very little cooking and parsimonious seasoning.*

## Sea Urchins in Thick Sauce

*20–30 sea urchins*
*1 small bay leaf*
*¼ t. ground pepper*
*1 t. honey*
*1 c. sea urchin or fish stock*
*1 raw egg yolk*
*(pepper)*

Simmer the sea urchins in water for 5 minutes. Drain, reserve liquid, and put them in a fresh pan.

For the sauce, combine bay leaf, pepper, honey, and stock. Heat, simmer for 10 minutes, remove bay leaf, and thicken with well beaten egg.

Serve the sea urchins in the sauce, with a sprinkling of pepper if you wish.

## Mussels in Savory Wine

*4 c. mussels in the shell*

Clean the mussels and cook them until the shells open. Drain and reserve stock.

*Sauce:*
*1 c. mussel stock, strained*
*2 T. chopped chives*
*¼ t. cumin*
*½ t. savory*
*¼ c. white wine*

For the sauce, combine the stock, chives, cumin to taste, savory, and white wine. Add to the mussels, and simmer together for 15 minutes before serving. *If you have the choice, use summer savory.*

## Stuffed Sardines

*10 fresh sardines*

Open the sardines and remove the backbones.

*Stuffing:*
*pinch of pennyroyal (or mint)*
*⅛ t. cumin*
*1½ t. mint*
*¼ c. finely chopped almonds*
*or other nuts*
*2 t. honey*
*foil or greaseproof paper*
*½ c. water*
*½ c. fish-pickle (see p. 2)*

To make the stuffing, combine pennyroyal (or mint), cumin, pepper, mint, and nuts. Bind with honey. Fill the sardines with this stuffing, and wrap in foil or greaseproof paper. Steam gently in water in a covered steamer for 30 minutes.

*Serve with fish-pickle, and a spinach and celery salad for two.*

## Sweet, Stuffed Sardines with Eggs

*10 fresh sardines*

*Stuffing:*
*¼ t. ground pepper*
*½ t. celery seed (or lovage)*
*¼ t. thyme*
*¼ t. oregano*
*pinch of rosemary (or rue)*
*¼ c. finely chopped dates*
*1 t. honey*
*eggs, hard-boiled*
*½ c. fish-pickle (see p. 2)*

Open the sardines and remove the backbones.

To make the stuffing, combine pepper, celery seed (or lovage), thyme, oregano, rosemary (or rue), and dates. Bind with honey. Then stuff sardines and steam, as in the preceding recipe (*Stuffed Sardines*).

When done, unwrap the sardines and arrange them on a serving dish. Decorate with sliced eggs, and serve with fish-pickle.

## Onion Dressing for Cold Sardines

*¼ t. ground pepper*
*⅛ t. cumin*
*¼ t. oregano*
*1 mint leaf, finely chopped*
*2 T. chopped onion*
*1 t. dried onion*
*¾ c. olive oil or salad oil*
*3 T. white wine or cider vinegar*

In a mortar, grind together pepper, cumin, and oregano. Add to mint, onion, oil, and vinegar.

Serve as a dressing with chilled, baked, or steamed sardines.

Alternatively, place canned sardines in a colander and wash gently in cold water.

*Serve with the dressing, as an appetizer, with unsalted crackers or bread sticks, and a glass of white wine.*

## Sweet Dressing for Cold Sardines

*¼ t. ground pepper*
*⅛ t. cumin*
*¼ t. celery seed (or lovage)*
*1–2 t. liquid honey*
*1 hard-boiled egg, chopped*

Make the dressing as above, but substitute celery seed (or lovage) for the oregano and add honey to taste.

Garnish cold sardines with a sprinkling of chopped hard-boiled egg, and pour a little dressing over them.

## Date Sauce for Baked Tuna or Sardines

*1 lb. tuna or sardines*

*Sauce:*
*¼ t. ground pepper*
*1 t. lovage (or celery seed)*
*2 t. celery seed*
*1 t. mint*
*pinch of rosemary (or rue)*
*2 T. dates, finely chopped*
*1 t. honey*
*1 t. white wine vinegar or cider vinegar*
*¼ c. white wine*
*2 T. olive oil*
*1 c. fish stock*

In a mortar, grind together pepper, lovage (or celery seed), celery seed, mint, and a pinch of rosemary (or rue). Add to dates. Blend with honey, vinegar, white wine, olive oil, and stock. Bring to a boil, simmer for 25 minutes to reduce, and serve with chilled fish.

Alternatively, make a cold dressing using 1 c. of olive oil, ¼ c. of vinegar, 2 T. white wine, and the chopped dates and seasonings.

*This and the following two recipes for cold fish dressings also work wonderfully well as green salad dressings.*

## Sweet Cumin Dressing for Cold Fish Fillets

*2 lbs. cooked cold fish fillets*

*Dressing:*
*¼ t. ground pepper*
*1 t. celery seed (or lovage)*
*¼–½ t. cumin to taste*
*1 fresh mint leaf*
*pinch of rosemary (or rue)*
*2 T. chopped onion*
*1 T. finely chopped almonds*
*1 T. finely chopped dates*
*1 t. liquid honey*
*3 T. white wine vinegar or cider vinegar*
*⅛ t. ground mustard*
*⅓ c. olive oil*

In a mortar, grind together pepper, celery seed (or lovage), cumin, chopped mint, and rosemary (or rue). Combine with onion, almonds, dates, honey, vinegar, mustard, and olive oil.

*Serve chilled with cold fish fillets or in fish salads, or as a dressing for lettuce and spinach salads.*

## Sweet Oregano Dressing for Cold Fish Fillets

*2 lbs. cooked, cold fish fillets*

*Dressing:*
*¼ t. ground pepper*
*½ t. oregano*
*dash mustard seed (or colewort)*
*1 mint leaf*
*pinch of rosemary (or rue)*
*1 T. finely chopped almonds*
*1 T. finely chopped dates*
*1 t. liquid honey*
*⅓ c. olive oil*
*3 T. white wine vinegar or cider vinegar*
*⅛ t. ground mustard*

In a mortar, grind together pepper, oregano, mustard seed (or colewort), mint, and rosemary (or rue). Add almonds and dates, and blend with honey, olive oil, vinegar, and mustard.

Chill and serve with cold fish fillets or in fish salads.

## Onion Dressing for Cold Tuna

*1 lb. canned tuna or cooked, cold fish fillets*

*Dressing:*
*¼ t. ground pepper*
*1 t. celery seed (or lovage)*
*¼ t. cumin*
*1 mint leaf*
*pinch of rosemary (or rue)*
*3 t. chopped onion*
*1 T. finely chopped almonds*
*1 T. finely chopped dates*
*1 t. liquid honey*
*2 T. white wine vinegar or cider vinegar*
*⅛ t. ground mustard*
*⅓ c. olive oil*

In a mortar, grind pepper, celery seed (or lovage), cumin, mint, and rosemary (or rue). Add to onion, almonds and dates, and blend with honey, vinegar, mustard, and olive oil.

Chill and serve with cold tuna, cold cooked fillets, or in a fish salad.

## Almond and Wine Dressing for Cold Fish

*1 lb. cooked, cold fish fillets*
*⅛ t. cumin*
*¼ t. ground pepper*
*1 T. boiled white wine (see p. 3)*
*2 T. finely chopped almonds*
*2 T. white wine vinegar or cider vinegar*
*⅓ c. olive oil*

In a mortar, grind together cumin and pepper. Add to almonds, and mix with wine, vinegar, and olive oil.

Serve with cold fish fillets, or in fish salads.

## Baian Oysters in Spiced Broth

*2 c. very small or chopped oysters*
*2 c. mussels*
*½ c. sea urchins*
*1 c. roasted almonds, chopped*
*8 T. shellfish liquid*
*pinch of rosemary (or rue)*
*1 c. chopped celery*
*½ t. ground pepper*
*1 t. coriander*
*¼ c. boiled white wine (see p. 3)*
*fish stock*
*3 T. finely chopped dates*
*2 T. olive oil*

Combine oysters, mussels, the edible parts of sea urchins (the ovaries), and almonds. Put these ingredients into a deep pot and add shellfish liquid. Season with rosemary (or rue), celery, pepper, coriander, boiled white wine, sufficient stock to cover, dates, and olive oil. Cook over low heat for 40 minutes in the covered pan.

*Adding tomatoes and pieces of scorpion fish or rascasse will result in a classical bouillabaise. Had the Romans known of the tomato I am certain it would have assumed an important role in their cookery. I do not like to take very small oysters off our shores, and prefer to chop up fresh, large ones. These have a better flavor than the imported canned ones.*

# The Fisherman

## Herb Sauce for Fried Fish

*2 lbs. fried fish fillets*

*Sauce:*
*¼ t. ground pepper*
*⅛ t. cumin*
*¼ t. coriander*
*pinch of fennel*
*pinch of rosemary (or rue)*
*1 t. white or cider vinegar*
*3 dates, finely chopped*
*(1 t. honey)*
*⅓ c. white wine*
*2 t. olive oil or butter*
*⅔ c. fish stock*

In a mortar, grind pepper, cumin, coriander seeds, fennel, and rosemary (or rue). Moisten these seasonings with vinegar. Combine with dates, (honey, if you wish ) white wine, olive oil, and stock. Bring the mixture to a boil, and simmer for 25 minutes to reduce.

Pour over the fried fish, and serve with a sprinkling of pepper.

## Sauce for Poached Fish Fillets

*2 lbs. poached fish fillets*

*Sauce:*
*¼ t. ground pepper*
*1 t. celery seed (or lovage)*
*½ t. oregano*
*1 small onion, chopped*
*¼ c. pine nuts or*
*almonds, chopped*
*3 dates, finely chopped*
*1 t. honey*
*1 t. white wine vinegar or*
*cider vinegar*
*⅛ t. ground mustard*
*1 t. olive oil or butter*
*1½ c. fish stock*
*(raisins)*

In a mortar, grind together pepper, celery seed (or lovage), and oregano. Mix with onion, nuts, and dates. Combine with honey, vinegar, mustard, olive oil or butter, and stock. Bring to a boil and simmer for 25 minutes to reduce.

Add raisins to the sauce ingredients, if you wish, and serve over poached fillets.

## Egg Sauce for Poached Fish

*2 lbs. poached fish fillets*

*Sauce:*
*¼ t. ground pepper*
*1 t. celery seed (or lovage)*
*½ t. coriander*
*¼ t. savory*
*2 T. chopped onion*
*3 hard-boiled egg yolks, chopped*
*½ c. white wine*
*1 t. white wine vinegar or cider vinegar*
*1 T. olive oil or butter*
*1 c. fish stock*

In a mortar, grind pepper, celery seed (or lovage), coriander, and savory. Add to onion. Combine with the egg yolks, wine, vinegar, olive oil or butter, and stock. Bring to a boil and simmer for 25 minutes to reduce.

*The yolks lend color to this dish. Very good served with lightly steamed broccoli in a white cheese sauce.*

## Fish Steamed with Coriander

*2 lbs. fish fillets*
*1 t. coriander*
*sharp white vinegar*

In a mortar, grind coriander seeds. Sprinkle this seasoning over the fish fillets. Roll the fish (so coriander remains on the fish) and secure each fillet with toothpicks. Cook in a little water in a covered pan in a 300°F oven for 30 minutes. Serve fillets on a platter with a sprinkling of vinegar.

## Fish Poached with Anise

*2 lbs. fish fillets*
*water*
*1 t. coriander seed*
*pinch of aniseed*
*sharp white vinegar*

Put the fish fillets in a frying pan. Barely cover with water, and season with coriander and aniseed. Bring to a boil and simmer for about 10 minutes. Discard liquid and serve fillets with a sprinkling of vinegar.

*Whenever Apicius specified coriander seeds I have found the crushed ripe green ones are best of all.*

## Oregano Plum Sauce for Fish

*2 lbs. fish fillets*

*Sauce:*
*½ t. ground pepper*
*1 t. lovage (or celery seed)*
*¼ t. cumin*
*½ t. oregano*
*½ t. celery seed*
*2 T. chopped onion*
*3 pitted damsons or plums,*
*thinly sliced*
*1 t. honey or 2 T. mead*
*1 t. white wine vinegar or*
*cider vinegar*
*½ c. white wine*
*1 T. olive oil or butter*
*1 c. fish stock*

In a mortar, grind pepper, lovage (or celery seed), cumin, oregano, and celery seed. Mix with onion, damsons or plums, then add honey or mead, vinegar, white wine, olive oil or butter, and fish stock. Heat to a boil and simmer gently for 25 minutes to reduce. Then serve with the cooked fillets.

## Alexandrine Wine Sauce for Fish

*2 lbs. fish fillets*

*Sauce:*
*¼ t. ground pepper*
*1 t. celery seed (or lovage)*
*½ t. coriander*
*¼ c. dark raisins*
*¼ c. white wine*
*1 T. olive oil or butter*
*1 c. fish stock*

In a mortar, grind pepper, celery seed (or lovage), and coriander. Combine with raisins, and blend with wine, olive oil or butter, and fish stock. Heat to a boil, and simmer gently for 25 minutes to reduce. Then serve with the cooked fillets.

*This is an exotic sauce in which the dark raisins sit attractively upon the white fish. Good served with small boiled potatoes sprinkled with parsley, or with rice.*

## Alexandrine Plum Sauce for Baked Fish

2 lbs. baked fish fillets

Sauce:
¼ t. ground pepper
1 t. celery seed (or lovage)
½ t. coriander
2 T. chopped onion
6 pitted damsons or plums,
sliced (or ¼ c. raisins)
¼ c. sweet white wine
1 t. white wine vinegar or
cider vinegar
1 T. olive oil or butter
1 c. fish stock

In a mortar, grind together pepper, celery seed (or lovage), and coriander. Add to onion. Combine with damsons, plums (or raisins), and mix with wine, vinegar, olive oil or butter, and fish stock. Heat to a boil and simmer gently for 25 minutes to reduce.

Serve with baked fish fillets.

## Egg Sauce for Baked Eel

2 lbs. baked eel

Sauce:
½ t. ground pepper
1 t. celery seed (or lovage)
¼ t. cumin
½ t. oregano
2 T. chopped onion
¼ c. white wine
1 t. honey or 2 T. mead
1 c. fish stock
1 t. white wine vinegar or
cider vinegar
3 hard-boiled eggs, chopped

In a mortar, grind together pepper, celery seed (or lovage), cumin, and oregano. Then blend with onion, wine, honey or mead, fish stock, and vinegar to taste. Bring to a boil, then simmer gently for 25 minutes to reduce.

Pour sauce over pieces of baked eel, and garnish with chopped eggs.

*This delicious, exotic sauce is best served over fish fillets on a bed of steamed rice.*

## Raisin Sauce for Poached Fish

*2 lbs. poached fish fillets*

*Sauce:*
*½ t. ground pepper*
*1 t. celery seed (or lovage)*
*½ t. oregano*
*1 T. chopped onion*
*¼ c. dark raisins*
*¼ c. white wine*
*1 t. honey*
*1 t. white wine vinegar or cider vinegar*
*½ c. fish stock*
*1 T. olive oil or butter*

In a mortar, grind pepper, celery seed (or lovage), and oregano. Combine with onion and raisins, and blend with wine, honey, vinegar, fish stock, and olive oil or butter.

Poach the fish fillets with the sauce for 10 minutes, and serve in the sauce.

## Nut Sauce for Baked Trout or Red Mullet

*3 lbs. whole baked trout or red mullet*

*Sauce:*
*½ t. ground pepper*
*1 t. celery seed (or lovage)*
*pinch of rosemary (or rue)*
*1 t. honey*
*¼ c. almonds, chopped*
*1 t. white wine vinegar or cider vinegar*
*2 T. white wine*
*¾ c. fish stock*
*1 t. olive oil or butter*

In a mortar, grind pepper, celery seed (or lovage), and rosemary (or rue). Combine with honey, nuts, vinegar, wine, fish stock, and olive oil or butter. Heat to a boil and simmer gently 25 minutes to reduce.

Serve with baked trout or red mullet.

*Delicious served with baked trout or red mullet, on a bed of steamed rice.*

## Honey Mint Sauce for Baked Trout or Mullet

*3 lbs. whole baked trout or red mullet*

*Sauce:*
*pinch of rosemary (or rue)*
*1 t. mint*
*½ t. coriander*
*pinch of fennel seed*
*½ t. ground pepper*
*1 t. celery seed (or lovage)*
*2 t. honey*
*1 c. fish stock*
*1 t. olive oil*
*3 T. white wine*

In a mortar, grind rosemary (or rue), mint, coriander, fennel seed, pepper, and celery seed (or lovage). Combine with honey, fish stock, olive oil, and white wine. Heat to a boil, then simmer gently for 25 minutes to reduce.

Serve with baked trout or red mullet.

*This sauce is understated so as not to overcome the trout's natural flavor, but everyone's taste is different. You may wish to accent the rosemary. I like it crushed in the hand and sprinkled into the pot. Others may take a long sprig and throw it in. Serve beside fresh peas sweetened with honey and seasoned with thyme.*

⟨When the city of Rome was at the zenith of her power in the first century A.D., the mullet held pride of place at the tables of the very rich. Their pursuit of this luxury can only be described as an obsession.

*Calliodorus, yesterday you sold a slave for 1,200 sesterces*
  *To dine well once.*
*But you didn't eat well: the 4 lb mullet you bought*
  *Was the spectacle, the chief dish of your dinner.*
*I cried out to you: "This is not a fish, you bastard, it's not:*
  *It's a man, Calliodorus, you've been eating a man."*
Martial.

When the craze for red mullet threatened to undermine the economic health of the city, Tiberius Caesar imposed a sumptuary tax on its sale in the markets, and this excellent fish once again assumed its proper place.

ALITER IUS IN MULLOS ASSOS  *Another Sauce for Baked Red Mullet*  Take rue, mint, coriander, fennel. [Make sure that these herbs are] all fresh. Add pepper, lovage, honey, fish stock, and a little olive oil.

IUS IN PELAMYDE ASSA  *Sauce for Baked Young Tunnyfish*  [Mix] pepper, lovage, oregano, green coriander, onion, pitted raisins, raisin wine, vinegar, fish stock, boiled wine, and olive oil. Cook. If you wish, add some honey. This sauce may also be served with poached [tunnyfish].

IUS IN PERCAM  *Sauce for Perch*  Pepper, lovage, fried cumin, onion, pitted damsons, wine, honey wine, vinegar, olive oil, and boiled wine. Cook.

IUS IN PISCE RUBELLIONE  *Sauce for Redfish*  Pepper, lovage, caraway, wild thyme, celery seed, dried onion, wine, raisin wine, vinegar, fish stock, and olive oil. Thicken with cornstarch.

For the Mediterranean tunnyfish we in North America may substitute the Californian tunny or tuna. Though the immature tuna is not commonly available, canned tuna can be used in its place. It should be drained, rinsed, moistened with a little melted butter, seasoned with coriander, and then baked in foil. The hot sauce is then poured over the cooked tuna at the table.

## Onion Raisin Sauce for Baked Tuna

*1 lb. baked tuna*

*Sauce:*
*¼ t. ground pepper*
*½ t. coriander*
*1 t. celery seed (or lovage)*
*½ t. oregano*
*1 t. white wine vinegar or cider vinegar*
*2 T. olive oil or butter*
*2 T. boiled white wine (see p. 3)*
*2 T. sweet raisin wine or muscatel*
*1 c. fish stock*
*2 T. chopped onion*
*¼ c. dark raisins*

In a mortar, grind together pepper, coriander, celery seed (or lovage), and oregano. Blend with vinegar, olive oil, boiled wine, sweet wine, and fish stock. Add onion and raisins. Heat to a boil, then simmer gently for 25 minutes to reduce.

Pour the cooked sauce over baked tuna.

This sauce, served with baked, canned tuna and a thick slice of French bread and butter, makes an exciting lunch.

*This sauce, served with baked, canned tuna and a thick slice of French bread and butter, makes an exciting lunch.*

## Wine Sauce for Poached Perch

*2–3 lbs. poached perch*

*Sauce:*
*¼ t. ground pepper*
*1 t. celery seed (or lovage)*
*¼ t. cumin*
*1 t. chopped onion*
*3 pitted damsons or plums,*
*thinly sliced*
*¼ c. white wine*
*1 t. white or cider vinegar*
*1 T. olive oil or butter*
*2 T. boiled wine (see*
*p. 3)*
*1 c. fish stock*
*(2 T. mead or 1 t. honey)*

In a mortar, grind together pepper, celery seed (or lovage), and cumin. Combine with onion and sliced plums. Mix with white wine, mead or honey, vinegar, olive oil or butter, boiled wine, fish stock, and, if you wish, mead or honey.

Bring to a boil, then simmer gently for 25 minutes to reduce.

Serve the sauce over each portion of poached fish.

*This recipe is a great favorite with many people. It also goes very well with freshly caught bass.*

## Caraway Sauce for Baked Salmon

*2 lbs. baked salmon*

*Sauce:*
*¼ t. ground pepper*
*1 t. lovage (or celery seed)*
*½ t. thyme*
*½ t. celery seed*
*pinch of caraway*
*1 T. chopped onion*
*¼ c. white wine*
*1 t. white wine vinegar or*
*cider vinegar*
*1 T. olive oil or butter*
*1 c. fish stock*
*flour*

In a mortar, grind together pepper, lovage (or celery seed), thyme, and celery seed. Add caraway and onion. Mix with white wine, vinegar, olive oil or butter, and fish stock. Bring to a boil, simmer gently for 20 minutes, then thicken with flour.

Serve the sauce over each portion of salmon.

*The delicate pink flesh of fresh salmon responds very well to this subtle caraway sauce. I like to serve it with steamed broccoli in a cream sauce that has been given a little character by adding lovage (or celery leaves) and parsley.*

## Saffron Wine Sauce for Poached Eels

*2 lbs. poached eels*

*Sauce:*
*½ t. ground pepper*
*1 t. celery seed (or lovage)*
*½ t. savory*
*pinch of saffron*
*1 T. chopped onion*
*3 pitted damsons or plums,*
*thinly sliced*
*¼ c. white wine*
*2 t. white wine vinegar or*
*cider vinegar*
*1 c. fish stock*
*1 T. olive oil*

In a mortar, grind together pepper, celery seed (or lovage), savory, and saffron. Add onion and sliced plums. Mix with white wine, vinegar, fish stock, and olive oil. Bring to a boil, then simmer gently for 25 minutes to reduce.

Serve the sauce with slices of poached eel.

*Because of their appearance eels have been much maligned. But their flesh, when properly seasoned as here, is delicious.*

## Plum Sauce for Poached Eels

*2 lbs. poached eels*

*Sauce:*
*½ t. ground pepper*
*½ t. celery seed (or lovage)*
*3 pitted damsons or plums,*
*thinly sliced*
*¼ c. white wine*
*2 t. white wine vinegar or*
*cider vinegar*
*1 c. fish stock*
*1 T. olive oil*

In a mortar, grind together pepper and celery seed (or lovage). Mix with sliced plums, wine, vinegar, stock, and olive oil.

Bring to a boil, then simmer gently for 25 minutes to reduce.

Serve the sauce with slices of poached eel.

## Onion Nut Sauce for Poached Eels

*2 lbs. poached eels*
*¼ t. ground pepper*
*½ t. celery seed (or lovage)*
*1 t. mint*
*10 coriander seeds*
*1 T. chopped onion*
*¼ c. pine nuts or chopped almonds*
*1 t. honey*
*2 t. white wine vinegar or cider vinegar*
*1 c. fish stock*
*1 T. olive oil*

In a mortar, grind together pepper, celery seed (or lovage), mint, and coriander. Add onion and nuts, and mix with honey, vinegar, fish stock, and olive oil. Bring to a boil, then simmer gently for 25 minutes to reduce. Serve the sauce over slices of poached eel.

## Anise Sauce for Poached Eels

*2 lbs. poached eels*

*Sauce:*
*¼ t. ground pepper*
*1 t. celery seed (or lovage)*
*pinch of aniseed*
*⅛ t. ground mustard*
*½ t. celery seed*
*3 dates, finely chopped*
*1 t. honey*
*2 t. white wine vinegar or cider vinegar*
*1 c. fish stock*
*1 T. olive oil or butter*
*¼ c. white wine*

In a mortar, grind together pepper, lovage (or celery seed), mustard, and celery seed. Combine with aniseed and dates. Mix with honey, vinegar, fish stock, olive oil, and wine.

Bring to a boil, then simmer gently for 25 minutes to reduce.

Serve the sauce over slices of poached eel.

## Cumin Sauce for Poached Fish Fillets

*2 lbs. poached fish fillets*

*Sauce:*
*⅛ t. ground pepper*
*1 t. celery seed (or lovage)*
*½ t. cumin*
*pinch of rosemary (or rue)*
*1 T. chopped onion*
*1 t. honey*
*1 t. white wine vinegar or cider vinegar*
*1 c. fish stock*
*1 T. olive oil*
*(flour)*

In a mortar, grind together pepper, celery seed (or lovage), cumin, and rosemary (or rue). Add to onion, and blend with honey, vinegar, stock, and olive oil. Bring the sauce to a boil, and simmer gently for 25 minutes to reduce. Thicken with flour, if you wish, and serve over cooked fillets.

## Parsley Sauce for Poached Fish Fillets

*2 lbs. poached fish fillets*

*Sauce:*
*¼ t. ground pepper*
*1 t. celery seed (or lovage)*
*4 T. fresh parsley, finely chopped*
*1 t. oregano*
*1 T. chopped onion*
*1 t. honey*
*1 c. fish stock*
*2 T. white wine*
*1 T. olive oil*
*(flour)*

In a mortar, grind together pepper, celery seed (or lovage), parsley, and oregano. Add to onion, and combine with honey, stock, wine, and olive oil. Bring the sauce to a boil, then simmer gently for 25 minutes to reduce. Thicken with flour, if you wish, and serve over poached fillets.

*Pour this parsley sauce liberally over fillets of poached fresh cod, plaice, or hake, and serve with boiled potatoes, and peas cooked with a little honey and thyme.*

## Thyme Sauce for Poached Fish Fillets

*2 lbs. poached fish fillets*

*Sauce:*
*½ t. ground pepper*
*1 t. celery seed (or lovage)*
*¾ t. thyme*
*¼ t. coriander*
*1 t. honey*
*1 t. white wine vinegar or cider vinegar*
*1 c. fish stock*
*¼ c. white wine*
*pinch of crushed rosemary (or sage)*
*(flour)*

In a mortar, grind together pepper, celery seed (or lovage), thyme, and coriander. Combine with honey, vinegar, stock, and wine. Heat these ingredients to a boil, adding a pinch of rosemary or, if you prefer, sage, then simmer for 25 minutes to reduce.

Thicken with flour, if you wish, and serve over cooked fillets.

*Very good served with carrots and boiled potatoes. Finish the meal with* Peaches Cooked with Cumin *(and mint and savory).*

## Coriander Sauce for Canned Tuna

*1 lb. canned tuna*

*Sauce:*
*¼ t. ground pepper*
*¼ t. cumin*
*½ t. thyme*
*½ t. coriander*
*1 T. chopped onion*
*2 T. dark raisins*
*1 t. honey*
*¼ c. white wine*
*2 T. olive oil*
*¾ c. fish stock*
*(flour)*

In a mortar, grind together pepper, cumin, thyme, and coriander. Add to onion and raisins, and mix with honey, white wine, olive oil, and stock. Heat to a boil and simmer gently for 25 minutes to reduce. Thicken with flour, if you wish, and serve with canned tuna.

## Date and Thyme Sauce for Poached Tuna

*1 lb. poached tuna*

*Sauce:*
*¼ t. ground pepper*
*½ t. celery seed (or lovage)*
*½ t. thyme*
*1 T. chopped onion*
*2 dates, finely chopped*
*1 t. honey*
*1 t. white wine vinegar or cider vinegar*
*2 t. olive oil*
*⅛ t. ground mustard*
*1 c. fish stock*

In a mortar, grind together pepper, celery seed (or lovage), thyme, and mustard. Combine with onion, chopped dates, honey, vinegar, olive oil, and stock. Bring to a boil, then simmer gently for 25 minutes to reduce.

Serve with the cooked fish.

## Pear or Quince Sauce for Baked Bluegill

*2–3 lb. baked bluegill*

*Sauce:*
*¼ t. ground pepper*
*½ t. celery seed (or lovage)*
*¼ t. coriander*
*1 t. mint*
*pinch of rosemary (or rue)*
*¼ c. diced, cooked pear or quince*
*1 t. honey*
*½ c. white wine*
*1 T. olive oil*
*2 c. fish stock*

In a mortar, grind together pepper, celery seed (or lovage), coriander, mint, and rosemary (or rue). Combine with pear or quince, honey, wine, olive oil, and stock. Bring to a boil, then simmer gently for 25 minutes to reduce.

Serve with the baked fish.

## Rosemary-Mint Sauce for Poached Bluegill

*2–3 lb. poached bluegill*

*Sauce:*
*½ t. ground pepper*
*pinch of aniseed*
*¼ t. cumin*
*½ t. thyme*
*1 t. fresh or dried mint*
*pinch of rosemary (or rue)*
*1 t. honey*
*1 t. white wine vinegar or cider vinegar*
*½ c. white wine*
*1 T. olive oil*
*1 c. fish stock*
*(flour)*

In a mortar, grind together pepper, aniseed, cumin, thyme, mint, and rosemary (or rue). Combine with honey, vinegar, white wine, olive oil, and stock. Bring to a boil and simmer gently to reduce for 25 minutes.

Thicken with flour, if you wish, and serve with the poached fish.

## Thick Myrtle Berry Sauce for Poached Bluegill

*2–3 lb. poached bluegill*

*Sauce:*
*¼ t. ground pepper*
*½ t. celery seed (or lovage)*
*½ t. oregano*
*pinch of rosemary (or rue)*
*1 t. myrtle berries*
*½ t. mint*
*pinch of caraway*
*1 t. honey*
*1 t. white or cider vinegar*
*1 T. olive oil*
*½ c. white wine*
*2 c. fish stock*
*2 raw egg yolks*

In a mortar, grind together pepper, celery seed (or lovage), oregano, rosemary (or rue), myrtle berries, and mint. Add caraway, and combine with honey, vinegar, olive oil, wine, and stock. Bring to a boil, simmer gently for 25 minutes, then thicken with well beaten yolks.

Serve with the poached fish.

*If you cannot obtain myrtle berries, substitute peppercorns but reduce the quantity.*

## Celery Mint Sauce for Baked Bluegill

*2–3 lbs. poached bluegill*

*Sauce:*
*½ t. ground pepper*
*½ t. coriander*
*½ t. mint*
*¼ c. chopped celery*
*1 T. chopped onion*
*2 T. dark raisins*
*1 t. honey*
*1 t. white or cider vinegar*
*1 T. olive oil*
*¼ c. white wine*
*1 c. fish stock*

In a mortar, grind together pepper, coriander, and mint. Mix with celery, onion, raisins, honey, vinegar, olive oil, white wine, and stock. Bring to a boil, then simmer gently for 25 minutes to reduce. Serve with the poached fish.

## Caraway Date Sauce for Poached Fish Fillets

*2 lbs. poached fish fillets*

*Sauce:*
*½ t. ground pepper*
*pinch of caraway*
*⅛ t. ground mustard*
*1 T. fresh parsley*
*¼ c. dates, finely chopped*
*1 t. honey*
*¾ c. fish stock*
*1 t. white or cider vinegar*
*1 T. olive oil*
*¼ c. boiled white wine (see wine sauce, p. 3)*

In a mortar, grind together pepper, caraway, mustard, and chopped parsley. Blend with dates, honey, stock, vinegar, olive oil, and wine. Bring to a boil, then simmer gently for 25 minutes to reduce. Serve with the poached fish.

℃ Of Vinidarius nothing is known except these records, which he made of
Apicius' work in the late fourth or early fifth centuries A.D.

## Vegetable and Chicken Casserole

*2–3 lbs. chicken*
*1 large stalk of broccoli, sliced*
*1 c. whole mushrooms*
*1 c. carrots, sliced*
*½ c. peas*
*½ t. ground coriander*
*1 t. ground pepper*
*1 bay leaf*
*1 t. thyme*
*2 t. celery seed (or lovage)*
*2 c. chicken stock*
*2 raw egg yolks*

Simmer the chicken in water for about 2½ hours. Then cut up, skin, and bone it, and put the meats in a large casserole. Add broccoli, mushrooms, carrots, and peas. Season with coriander, ground pepper, bay leaf, thyme, and celery seed (or lovage). Take well beaten egg yolks and combine with stock. Pour over the casserole, cover it, and cook in a 350°F oven for 30–40 minutes.

## Chicken, Pork, and Vegetables in Custard

*½ lb. cooked chicken, sliced*
*½ lb. cooked pork, sliced*
*½ c. peas*
*1 large stalk of broccoli, sliced*
*2 heads of leeks, chopped*
*1 c. whole small beets*
*1 c. green beans, sliced*
*1 t. ground pepper*
*2 t. celery seed (or lovage)*
*1 t. thyme*
*½ t. sage*
*½ t. coriander*
*2 T. butter*
*¼ c. white wine*
*1 T. honey*
*1½ c. chicken stock*
*2 c. milk*
*2 raw egg yolks*

Arrange the meats and vegetables in layers in a greased casserole. In a mortar, grind together pepper, celery seed (or lovage), thyme, sage, and coriander. Melt butter and blend with wine, honey, and stock. Scald the milk. Beat the yolks and add the milk little by little to the eggs. Then mix with the wine sauce. Now add the seasonings and stir well. Heat over low heat, stirring till partly thickened. Then pour the custard over the casserole, and bake, uncovered, in a 350°F oven for 45 minutes to 1 hour, or until the custard has set.

OFELLAS GARATAS *Hors D'oeuvres Made with Fish-pickle* Put pieces of meat into a frying pan. Add a measure of fish-pickle, similarly [a measure] of olive oil, some honey, and fry.

OFELLAS ASSAS *Roast Hors D'oeuvres* Prepare the roasted morsels of choice meat carefully and put them in a frying pan. Fry in wine sauce. Afterwards, serve in the very same wine sauce and sprinkle with pepper.

ALITER OFELLAS *Another Hors D'oeuvre* Fry the pieces of meat in fish-pickle. When hot, smear [each] with honey, and serve.

OFELLAS GARATON *Hors D'oeuvres Made with Fish-pickle* Take laser, ginger, and cardamon, and mix one-eighth of a pint of stock with all of these ground seasonings. Cook the pieces of meat in this [sauce].

The Poet Martial's Lament

*Full glasses of Setine strained through snow,*\*
*When shall I drink you again, without my doctor saying no?*

Martial.

---

\*Setine wine, like many other great classical Italian wines, was strained through snow both to cool it and to dilute its strength.

## Meat Hors D'oeuvres with Fish-pickle

*½ lb. choice cooked beef, pork, lamb, or kid*
*2 T. olive oil*
*¼ c. fish-pickle (see p. 2)*
*¼ c. liquid honey*

Cut thinly sliced meat into 1 inch squares, and sauté on each side in olive oil. Brush each piece with honey, and season with ½ teaspoon fish-pickle.

*These hors d'oeuvres are excellent served on squares of toast.*

## Roast Meat Morsels in Wine Sauce

*½ lb. choice roast beef, pork, lamb, or kid*

*Sauce:*
*½ c. red wine*
*½ c. beef stock*
*pinch of rosemary*
*1 t. celery seed (or lovage)*
*½ t. coriander*
*⅛ t. basil*
*1 t. honey*

Thinly slice roast meat, and cut into 1 inch squares. Combine wine and beef stock, and season with rosemary, celery seed (or lovage), coriander, and basil. Add honey. Bring to a boil, then simmer the morsels of meat in it for 15 minutes.

Serve the pieces of meat in a little of the sauce, with a sprinkling of pepper.

## Spiced Roast Meat Hors D'oeuvres

*½ lb. choice roast beef, pork, lamb, or kid*

*Sauce:*
*¼ t. ginger*
*pinch of cardamon*
*pinch of fennel*
*¼ c. beef stock*
*2 T. olive oil*

Take cooked meat and slice into thin 1 inch squares. In a mortar, grind together ginger, cardamon, and fennel. Moisten each slice with stock, and season with the spices. Sauté briefly in olive oil in a very hot frying pan.

## Fish Fillets with Turnips in Saffron Sauce

2 lbs. fish fillets
1 c. fish stock
1 T. olive oil
6 medium turnips

Sauce:
½ t. cumin
a few crushed laurel berries,
or ¼ t. ground pepper
¼ c. white wine
1 t. honey
¾ c. fish stock
1 T. olive oil or butter
1 T. flour
pinch of saffron
white wine vinegar or
cider vinegar

To make this dish, peel turnips, and cook until soft. Mash them, and spread the paste on a serving platter. Take fish fillets and poach them lightly in stock and a little olive oil. Place the cooked fillets on top of the mashed turnips, season with the saffron sauce below, and serve with a sprinkling of pepper.

For the sauce, grind together cumin and laurel berries or pepper. Combine with white wine, honey, stock, and olive oil or butter. Bring to a boil, simmer for 25 minutes, and thicken with flour. Add saffron for color. Pour the sauce over the cooked fillets and serve with a sprinkling of vinegar.

*Although this sauce is excellent, fish fillets coated in turnip paste and deep fried are satisfying in themselves.*

## Date Sauce for Fried or Poached Fish Fillets

2 lbs. fried fish or poached
fillets

Sauce:
¼ t. ground pepper
½ t. coriander
pinch of fennel
½ t. oregano
pinch of rosemary (or rue)
2 dates, finely chopped
1 t. white wine vinegar or
cider vinegar
1 t. olive oil
¾ c. fish stock
¼ c. boiled white wine

In a mortar, grind together pepper, coriander, fennel, oregano, rosemary (or rue). Add to chopped dates. Moisten with vinegar and olive oil, and combine with stock and boiled wine. Bring to a boil and simmer for 25 minutes to reduce.

Serve with cooked fish and a sprinkling of pepper.

## Coriander Sauce for Fried or Poached Fish

*2 lbs. fried or poached fish fillets*

*Sauce:*
*¼ t. ground pepper*
*1 t. celery seed (or lovage)*
*½ t. coriander*
*1 t. honey*
*¼ c. white wine*
*¾ c. fish stock*
*1 whole bay leaf*
*flour*

In a mortar, grind together pepper, celery seed, (or lovage), and coriander. Blend with honey, white wine, and fish stock. Add bay leaf. Bring to a boil and simmer gently for 25 minutes. Remove bay leaf and thicken with flour.

Pour over cooked fish, and serve.

## Aniseed Sauce for Baked Salmon

*2–3 lbs. salmon, baked*

*Sauce:*
*¼ t. ground pepper*
*1 t. celery seed (or lovage)*
*½ t. savory*
*2 T. chopped onion*
*2 t. white or cider vinegar*
*2 dates, finely chopped*
*pinch of aniseed*
*1 t. honey*
*1 c. fish stock*
*2 t. olive oil or butter*
*¼ c. boiled white wine (see p. 3)*
*1 raw egg yolk*

In a mortar, grind together pepper, celery seed (or lovage), and savory. Add to onion. Moisten these seasonings with vinegar. Combine with chopped dates, aniseed, honey, fish stock, olive oil, and boiled white wine. Bring to a boil, then simmer for 15 minutes, and thicken with well beaten egg yolk.

Serve over portions of baked salmon.

## Spiced Fish Stew

*2 lbs. fish fillets or steaks*
*2 c. water*
*½ t. ground pepper*
*2 t. celery seed (or lovage)*
*½ t. thyme*
*½ t. rosemary (or rue)*
*2 T. chopped onion*
*2 t. butter or olive oil*
*2 T. fish-pickle (see p. 2)*

Cover the fish in water and cook for 10–15 minutes. Pour off the liquid and reserve. In a mortar, grind together pepper, celery seed (or lovage), and rosemary (or rue). Add to onion, olive oil, and fish-pickle. Combine with the reserved stewing liquid, and pour back over the stewed fish. Cook together over low heat for 5 minutes, then serve.

## Dressing for Cold Sardines

*8 oz. plain canned sardines*

*Dressing:*
*¼ t. ground pepper*
*1 t. celery seed (or lovage)*
*½ t. oregano*
*2 T. chopped onion*
*3 hard-boiled egg yolks, finely chopped*
*3 T. white wine vinegar or cider vinegar*
*½ c. olive oil*

In a mortar, grind together pepper, celery seed (or lovage), and oregano. Add to onion. Combine with egg yolks, vinegar, and olive oil. Chill. Serve with the sardines after they have been drained and rinsed in cold water.

### Fish Stewed in Seasoned Wine

*2 lbs. uncooked fish fillets or steaks*
*1 c. fish stock*
*1 c. boiled white wine (see p. 3)*
*1 T. olive oil*
*2 heads of leeks, sliced*
*1 t. coriander*
*½ t. ground pepper*
*1–2 t. celery seed (or lovage)*
*2 raw egg yolks*

Chop fillets into pieces, and put into a stewing pot. Add stock, boiled wine, olive oil, leeks, coriander, pepper, and celery seed (or lovage). Bring to a boil and simmer for 10–15 minutes. Then thicken the liquid by adding the well beaten egg yolks, little by little.

Serve with a sprinkling of pepper.

### Mullet Stewed with Aniseed

Prepare fish and liquid as in *Fish Stewed in Seasoned Wine*, above, adding a pinch of aniseed. In the sauce, omit oregano and celery seed (or lovage), and add 1 teaspoon white or cider vinegar.

## Trout in Thickened Wine Sauce

*2 lbs. trout*
*1 t. olive oil*
*3 T. fish-pickle (see p. 2)*
*1 T. white wine*
*2 T. chives, finely chopped*
*½ t. coriander*

Clean the insides of the fish, and season with a mixture of olive oil, fish-pickle, white wine, chives, and coriander. Then sauté trout, till done, in olive oil or butter.

*Sauce:*
*¼ t. ground pepper*
*½ t. mint*
*½ t. thyme*
*a pinch of aniseed*
*2 t. olive oil or butter*
*1 t. white wine vinegar or cider vinegar*
*1 T. sweet white wine or muscatel*
*1 c. fish stock*
*flour*

For the sauce, grind together pepper, mint, and thyme. Add aniseed. Combine with olive oil or butter, vinegar, sweet wine, and stock. Bring to a boil, then simmer for 25 minutes, and thicken with flour. Serve over the hot, cooked trout.

## Eels Poached in Sweet Sauce

*2 lbs. eels*

*Sauce:*
*¼ t. ground pepper*
*1 t. celery seed (or lovage)*
*½ t. oregano*
*½ t. mint*
*2 T. chopped onion*
*1 t. honey*
*¼ c. boiled white wine (see p. 3)*
*1 c. fish stock*

Arrange pieces of eel in a stewing pan. In a mortar, grind together pepper, celery seed (or lovage), oregano, and mint. Add to onion. Blend with honey, boiled wine, and stock, and pour into the pan with the eels. Bring sauce to a boil and simmer over low heat for 30 minutes, or until done.

## Celery Seed Sauce for Lobsters or Prawns

*2 c. cooked shellfish meats*

*Sauce:*
*¼ t. ground pepper*
*2 t. lovage (or celery seed)*
*1 t. white wine vinegar or*
*cider vinegar*
*1 c. shellfish liquid*
*1 raw egg yolk*

In a mortar, grind together pepper and celery seed (or lovage). Combine with vinegar and liquid from the boiled shellfish. Bring to a boil and simmer for 25 minutes. Then add well beaten egg yolk little by little to thicken.

Serve with cooked lobster or prawns.

## Nut Sauce for Poached Fish Fillets

*2 lbs. poached fish fillets*

*Sauce:*
*¼ t. ground pepper*
*1 t. lovage (or celery seed)*
*1 t. celery seed*
*½ t. oregano*
*1 t. white wine vinegar or*
*cider vinegar*
*¼ c. pine nuts, chopped, or*
*almonds, thinly sliced*
*2 dates, finely chopped*
*1 t. honey*
*1 c. fish stock*
*1 t. white or cider vinegar*
*¼ t. ground mustard*
*vinegar*

In a mortar, grind together pepper, lovage (or celery seed), celery seed, and oregano. Moisten these seasonings with vinegar, and combine with nuts, dates, honey, fish stock, vinegar, and mustard. Bring to a boil, then simmer to reduce for 25 minutes.

Pour over poached fish and serve with a sprinkling of vinegar.

## Fillet of Sole Omelette

*1 lb. fillets of sole*
*2 T. olive oil or butter*
*2–3 T. fish-pickle (see p. 2)*
*1 T. chives, chopped*
*½ t. coriander*
*¼ t. ground pepper*
*½ t. oregano*
*4 raw eggs*
*½ c. milk*

Put olive oil or butter in a baking pan, and arrange fillets of sole in it. Season with fish-pickle, chives, and coriander. Cook in oven for 10 minutes at 300°F. Meanwhile, in a mortar, grind pepper and oregano. Combine juices from the pan of fillets, with well beaten eggs, and milk. Blend and pour into a greased frying pan, and add the fish. Cook the omelette until it is firm, sprinkle with pepper, and *Serve for lunch with a spinach and almond salad.*

## Roast Pork

*4 lb. pork roast or suckling pig*
*1 t. cumin*

Sprinkle the roast with cumin, and roast uncovered for 2½ hours in a 325°F oven.

*Sauce:*
*½ t. ground pepper*
*1 t. oregano*
*1½ t. coriander*
*pinch of aniseed*
*1 T. honey*
*¼ c. red wine*
*1 c. beef or chicken stock*
*2 t. olive oil or butter*
*1 t. wine vinegar or cider vinegar*
*¹/₄ c. boiled red wine (see p. 3)*
*¹/₄ c. dark raisins*
*flour*
*¹/₄ c. almonds, chopped*
*1 small onion, finely chopped*
*¹/₄ c. coconut, finely chopped*

For the sauce, in a mortar, grind together pepper, oregano, and coriander. Add aniseed, and combine with honey, red wine, stock, olive oil or butter, vinegar, and boiled wine. After 2½ hours, pierce the roast here and there with a fork to release some of the juices into the pan. Add the prepared sauce to the pan, and baste from time to time for a further ½ hour. Thicken sauce with flour, and serve with slices of pork. Garnish with raisins, almonds, chopped onion, and coconut. (Although the Romans did not have the coconut, it makes a splendid addition to the garnish.)

*Precede this festive roast with* Cumin Spiced Artichokes, *then serve with saffron rice, and steamed carrots.*

## Pork Roast Stewed in Wine

*4 lb. choice loin roast or suckling pig*
*1 c. pork, beef, or chicken stock*
*2 T. olive oil or butter*

Roast the pork or suckling pig, uncovered, in a 325°F oven for 2½ hours, basting with a mixture of stock and olive oil or butter.

*Sauce:*
*½ t. ground pepper*
*3 cloves (or laurel berries)*
*½ c. pork, beef, or chicken stock*
*¼ c. sweet raisin wine or muscatel*
*¼ c. aged red wine*
*flour*

For the sauce, in a mortar, grind the pepper, and cloves (or laurel berries), and combine with stock, sweet wine, and red wine. Bring this sauce to a boil, then pour over roast, and cook together for another 30 minutes, basting occasionally. Strain out the cloves, and thicken the sauce with flour before serving.

## Roast Pork with Thyme

*4 lb. pork roast*
*1 t. thyme*

Take the roast and sprinkle it with thyme. Roast, uncovered, in a 325°F oven for 2½ hours.

*Sauce:*
*1 t. fresh chervil, chopped*
*½ t. mint*
*1 t. celery seed (or lovage)*
*1 t. thyme*
*pinch of pennyroyal (or mint)*
*1 onion, finely chopped*
*1 c. pork, beef, or chicken stock*
*2 t. olive oil or butter*
*¼ c. red wine*
*flour*
*1 onion, finely chopped*
*3 hard-boiled eggs, chopped*

Meanwhile, for the sauce, finely chop chervil, and combine with mint, celery seed (or lovage), thyme, and pennyroyal (or mint). Mix these herbs with onion, stock, olive oil or butter, and wine. Bring to a boil, then pour over the roast. Cook for a further ½ hour, basting occasionally. Then thicken sauce with flour.

Serve slices of meat with a little of the sauce and a garnish of chopped hard-boiled eggs and onion.

*If you like it, the quantity of thyme can be increased to a tablespoon. Rotate the roast in order to season the meat evenly. Very good served with firm, boiled potatoes, and a dish of peas sweetened with a little honey and topped with butter.*

## Roast Pork in Onion Coriander Sauce

*4 lb. pork roast*

Roast meat, uncovered, in a 325°F oven for 2½ hours.

*Sauce:*
*1 T. honey*
*3 large onions, chopped*
*2 t. coriander*
*1 c. pork, beef, or chicken stock*
*2 T. olive oil or butter*
*ground pepper*

Meanwhile, for the sauce, mix honey, chopped onions, coriander, stock, and olive oil or butter. Pour this sauce into the pan with the meat and mix it with pan juices. Cook together for a further ½ hour. Serve slices of meat with the sauce and a sprinkling of pepper.

*Very good when accompanied with* Pickled Beets *and broccoli in an Edam cheese sauce. Blackberries folded in whipped cream make a fine dessert.*

## Roast Pork or Suckling Pig in Cumin Sauce

*4 lb. pork roast*
*1 t. cumin*

Sprinkle cumin over the roast and cook, uncovered, in a 325°F oven for 2½ hours.

*Sauce:*
*½ t. ground pepper*
*1 t. celery seed (or lovage)*
*½ t. cumin*
*¼ t. fennel*
*1 t. white wine vinegar or cider vinegar*
*pinch of caraway*
*¼ c. pine nuts or almonds, chopped*
*¼ c. dates, chopped*
*1 T. honey*
*1½ c. pork, beef, or chicken stock*
*⅛ t. ground mustard*
*2 t. olive oil or butter*
*flour*
*ground pepper*

For the sauce, in a mortar, grind pepper, celery seed (or lovage), cumin, and fennel. Combine with vinegar, and add caraway, nuts, chopped dates, honey, stock seasoned with mustard, and olive oil or butter. Bring this sauce to a boil, add roasting pan juices, and simmer for 20 minutes. Thicken with flour and serve with a sprinkling of pepper.

*Serve with fresh green beans, steamed and buttered, and* Carrots Cooked with Cumin.

## Sweet Aniseed Sauce for Pork Roast

*4 lb. pork roast*

*Sauce:*
*¼ t. ground pepper*
*1 t. celery seed (or lovage)*
*¼ t. rosemary (or rue)*
*pinch of aniseed*
*2 cloves or laurel berries*
*1 c. pork, beef, or*
*chicken stock*
*1 head of leek, thinly sliced*
*¼ c. sweet white wine, or*
*muscatel, or 1 T. honey*
*¼ c. red wine*
*2 t. olive oil or butter*
*flour*

In a mortar, grind together pepper, celery seed (or lovage), and rosemary (or rue). Add aniseed and cloves or laurel berries. Combine with stock, sliced leek, sweet wine or honey, red wine, and olive oil or butter. Bring the sauce to a boil, simmer for 25 minutes, then remove cloves.

Thicken with flour, and serve with slices of roast pork.

## Lamb Chops in a Simple Sauce

*2 lbs. lamb chops*
*2 T. olive oil*

*Sauce:*
*2 heads of leeks, sliced*
*½ c. beef or chicken stock*
*¼ c. red wine*
*1½ t. coriander*
*1 t. mint*
*ground pepper*

In a pan, brown lamb chops in olive oil. Add sliced leeks, stock, red wine, coriander, and mint. Cook the lamb in this sauce for about 30 minutes, stirring repeatedly.

Serve in the sauce with a sprinkling of pepper.

*This recipe reminds me of Horace's poetic words—* simplex munditiis—*artfully simple.*

## Roast Kid Stuffed with Ginger Sausage

8–10 lb. kid
½ t. ground pepper
½–1 t. ginger
2 t. celery seed (or lovage)
½ t. cumin
2 T. olive oil or butter
1 c. finely ground pork or beef
1 c. calf's liver, chopped
1 T. butter
1 raw egg
2 c. bread crumbs
beef or chicken stock
four 8" sausage casings

Prepare the kid for roasting. For the stuffing, make sausages by filling casings with the following ingredients.

In a mortar, grind together pepper, ginger, celery seed (or lovage), and cumin. Add to olive oil or butter. Combine with ground meats, and calf's liver browned in butter. Bind the mixture with the well beaten egg and bread crumbs. Moisten with stock as required, before stuffing into sausage casings. Simmer the sausages in a little water in a covered pan for 20 minutes.

Stuff the kid with the cooked sausage, and roast in a 325°F oven for 4–5 hours.

*Serve with one of the sauces for meats. Delicious with* Alexandrine Squash *or* Steamed Squash Sautéed with Cumin, *and buttered peas, and a favorite full-bodied red wine.*

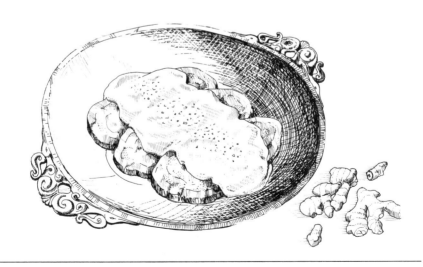

## Stuffed Cornish Hens in Wine Gravy

*2 cornish hens or 1 small roasting chicken*

In a mortar, grind together pepper, ginger, cloves (or juniper berries), and cumin. Add to fish-pickle, chicken livers, and ground pork. Bind with bread crumbs and well beaten egg. Stuff the birds with this mixture, and roast in oven till done.

*Seasoning:*
*¼ t. ground pepper*
*½ t. ginger*
*3 cloves (or juniper berries)*
*½ t. cumin*
*1 T. fish-pickle (see p. 2)*
*½ c. cooked chicken livers, chopped*
*¼ lb. ground pork*
*1 c. bread crumbs*
*1 raw egg*

*Gravy:*
*2 heads of leeks, finely chopped*
*1 t. celery seed (or lovage)*
*½ t. oregano*
*1 c. chicken stock*
*¼ c. white wine*
*2 T. finely chopped dates or dark raisins*
*2 T. olive oil or butter*
*flour*

Make the gravy by combining leeks, celery seed (or lovage), oregano, stock, wine, and dates or raisins. Add pan juices, bring to a boil, simmer slowly for 20 minutes, and thicken with flour.

*Like many Roman recipes for fowl, this one is so full of flavor that another highly spiced dish on the table would be superfluous, or excessive. I like to serve this dish with plain brown or wild rice, preceded with a lettuce and celery salad and followed with cheese, nuts, and coffee.*

## LIST OF SUBSTITUTIONS

These substitutions may be made without doing violence to the authenticity of the Roman recipes.

| *For:* | *Use:* |
| --- | --- |
| alecost | mint |
| chervil | aniseed |
| colewort | mustard seed |
| costmary | mint |
| cyperus root | ginger |
| Damascus plums | damsons |
| Egyptian bean root | taro root, potato |
| Egyptian beans | broad beans |
| elecampane | aniseed |
| fish-pickle | See p. 2. |
| hyssop | mint |
| laser | fennel or ginger (see recipes) |
| laurel berries (with fish) | peppercorns |
| laurel berries (with meat) | cloves or juniper berries |
| lovage | celery seed or dried celery leaves |
| mastic | cinnamon, pistachio nut extract, ground pistachios |
| myrtle berries (with fish) | peppercorns |
| myrtle berries (with meat) | cloves or juniper berries |
| pellitory | chamomile |
| pennyroyal | mint |
| rocket | mustard seed |
| rue | rosemary |
| rue berries | peppercorns |
| savory | oregano |
| silphium | fennel or ginger |
| spelt | fine flour |
| spikenard, Indian spikenard, European nard | bay leaf |

# INDEX

# Index

# Index

# Index